Library of English Renaissance Literature

PHILOSOPHY IN POETRY

Philosophy in Poetry

A STUDY OF SIR JOHN DAVIES'S POEM
"NOSCE TEIPSUM"

BY

ELIAS HERSHEY SNEATH

The proper study of mankind is man
POPE, *Essay on Man*

 BOOKS FOR LIBRARIES PRESS
FREEPORT, NEW YORK

First Published 1903
Reprinted 1970

STANDARD BOOK NUMBER:
8369-5408-4

LIBRARY OF CONGRESS CATALOG CARD NUMBER:
79-119965

PRINTED IN THE UNITED STATES OF AMERICA

The acquisition of knowledge is, we conceive, always something high and honourable : but one form of knowledge is superior to another either in virtue of the self-contained simplicity of its truths or by the greater dignity and wondrousness of its contents : and on both these grounds the investigation of the soul might with justice claim a foremost place.

ARISTOTLE, *De Anima*, trans. by Wallace, Bk. I., Ch. I., Sec. I.

PREFACE

SIR JOHN DAVIES'S philosophical poem, *Nosce Teipsum*, is regarded by competent critics as one of the finest pieces of philosophical verse in the English language. It is really a masterpiece of metrical philosophy. It is also of importance as furnishing an insight into the psychology and philosophy of the period immediately preceding the birth of modern philosophy. However, no interpretation of the poem, tracing its antecedents, unfolding its speculative contents, and giving them an historical setting, has ever been made by historian or essayist, either in English literature or in philosophy. The following Study aims to supply this deficiency. It is, therefore, hoped that it may prove to be a real contribution to the literature of both departments of learning, as well as of interest to the intelligent reader. As the poem is not easily accessible, it was deemed advisable to publish it as an appendix to the Study. The text is taken from Grosart's edition (London, 1876). It is to be regretted that a more carefully edited edition of the text is not available.

A study of the sources of Davies's philosophy was of course necessary for a scholarly treatment of the subject. Furthermore, it was thought that a statement of the position of the philosophical contents of the poem in the stream of speculative thought might be of special service to students of English literature. But the introduction of this material, at the close of the various chapters, has, to a certain extent, broken the continuity of the exposition. The only alternatives were to introduce this matter either as footnotes, or as notes at the end of the volume. After careful consideration, the method adopted seemed less distracting, and more in accord with the aim of the volume than the others.

The author gratefully acknowledges his obligations to his colleague, Professor Albert S. Cook, of Yale University, for valuable suggestions and criticism in the final revision of the work.

E. H. S.

YALE UNIVERSITY,
October, 1903.

CONTENTS

PHILOSOPHY IN POETRY

INTRODUCTION

IT is an interesting and noteworthy fact that
English poetry has, to a very large extent,
concerned itself with the problems of philosophy.
The careful student of English verse cannot fail
to be impressed by the fact that England's greatest
poets have been dependent, in no small measure,
upon these problems for poetical inspiration and
content. Beginning with Spenser, we find that he
presents, in the *Faery Queen*, an elaborate system
of social and moral philosophy. In a letter to
Sir Walter Raleigh he acknowledged this to be his
aim. And, as one reads this interesting and beautiful poem, noting the impersonation of the virtues
in its heroes, he can trace much of the poet's inspiration to the *Nicomachean Ethics* of Aristotle.
It would doubtless be drawing upon the imagination to speak of Shakespeare as formulating a system of philosophy. But it is certainly within the

bounds of truth to say, that rarely has any psychologist or moral philosopher portrayed the ethical
life, and its philosophical implications, with greater
accuracy and force than did he.   The supremacy
of conscience, the absoluteness of moral law, the
freedom of the human will, man's responsibility
for conduct, the implications of the moral nature
with reference to God and Destiny, these are subjects which engaged the genius of England's greatest poet, and which he treated with remarkable
insight.   Milton, like Dante, derived much inspiration from the problems of Christian philosophy.
Paradise Lost and *Paradise Regained* show that
a philosophy of evil, and a philosophy of redemp-
tion, inspired poetry which for grandeur and sublimity is hardly surpassed in the history of verse.
Pope chose the philosophical problems of man's
relation to the cosmos, his relation to himself, his
relation to society, and his conceptions of human
happiness, as the subjects of his chief poetical
work — the *Essay on Man*.   Among the main
sources of Shelley's early poetical inspiration was
an atheistic and anarchistic philosophy.   The very
soul of *Queen Mab* is a philosophy of negation.
And, later, in *Prometheus Unbound*, the questions
of social philosophy engaged his mind.   Words-

worth confessed himself ambitious to be a philosophic poet. A philosophy of nature as well as a philosophy of society seriously commanded his reflective and æsthetic powers. And Aubrey De Vere is not far afield in saying: "He is England's great philosophic, as Shakespeare is her great dramatic, and Milton her great epic, poet."[1] Coleridge did most of his philosophizing in prose. But it is interesting to note how intimately related are the æsthetic and reflective in his mind, and it is difficult to resist the conviction, that they were mutually helpful in his poetizing and philosophizing. Browning as a poet is greatly indebted to the problems of philosophy. Doubtless more of a dramatic psychologist than a philosopher, he nevertheless thought long and seriously on the profound problems of a philosophy of life; and much of his poetry is devoted to an expression of a philosophical optimism which is the result of his reflection. With regard to Tennyson, it has been shown elsewhere[2] that the questions of God, Freedom, and Immortality — "the inevitable problems," as Kant calls them — lie at the very roots

[1] Essays chiefly on Poetry. London and New York, 1887, Vol. I. p. 177.

[2] Sneath, "The Mind of Tennyson." New York, 1900.

of his poetry. They, more than any other subject, engaged his genius. And much of his power
over the hearts and minds of men is due to the
consummate manner in which he has given poetical
expression to his thought on these fundamental
questions.

What is true of English poetry in its relation
to the problems of philosophy, is true of the great
poetry of the world. The great poets of every
age and of every nation deal with the fundamental
problems of human thought and life. A careful
inquiry into the history of poetry — both ancient
and modern — reveals the fact that these vital
problems of thought and life have not been the
exclusive property of the philosopher and theologian, but that the poet also has a legitimate
claim upon them, having established it by the
fact that these problems have proven to be a
prolific source of poetic inspiration; an inex-
haustible storehouse of poetic content or subject-
matter.

Now if we examine the method of the poet's
dealing with these problems we shall find a twofold method revealed. The poet may be possessed of an intuitive power by which he gains
an almost immediate insight into the nature of

Truth and Reality. Or, like the average philosopher, he may reach a knowledge of such Truth and Reality by a long and carefully sustained process of reasoning. In the first case, we have intuitive philosophy; in the second, reasoned philosophy. In the first case, we have merely a record of intuitions, clothed often in highly imaginative and descriptive poetry. In the second case, we have philosophizing in verse — a statement of positions, and an elaborate poetical presentation of the process of reasoning by which those positions were attained. Undoubtedly the greater portion of philosophical poetry is of the intuitive order. It is an immediate envisagement of Truth and Reality. This is what we should naturally expect. The poet's mind, as a rule, proceeds synthetically rather than analytically and discursively, as do the minds of the scientist and philosopher. He grasps the unity in the manifold, the one in the many, generally by an act of poetic intuition rather than by a long process of analysis and generalization, or by a severe and sustained method of reasoning. As to whether his intuitions are as valid as are their generalizations reached by induction and deduction, individual opinions will differ. But some there be who will not deny that the heart of Reality may be pierced as truly by such intuition as by logical inference.

But all philosophical poetry is not of the intuitive order. There are poetic minds which, in their pursuit of ultimate Truth and Reality, proceed by the ordinary methods of philosophy — minds that really philosophize — that move by the slow, careful, and toilsome processes of reasoning to the attainment of knowledge; and, having reached conclusions by such methods, these are embodied in verse. These minds are, more strictly speaking, the philosophical poets. They are, however, undoubtedly aided by the poetic nature in their pursuit of truth in some other manner than by direct intuition, for cognition is not solely a matter of the intellectual nature of man. The æsthetic nature shares largely in the pursuit of knowledge. There are æsthetic momenta in human knowledge which superficial analysis is wont to overlook. Much of scientific generalization and philosophic conclusion is not mere inference from bare fact of experience. Such generalization and conclusion frequently carry us beyond what rigid logical inference would justify. Man enters upon the study of phenomena and Reality with conceptions of, and a love for, order, proportion, symmetry, and harmony — with æsthetic ideals and feelings — and insists that an interpretation of the facts of science, and the Reality of philosophy, satisfy these æsthetic elements of human nature. The history of science and philosophy bears testimony to the fact. Neither science nor philosophy can establish, by strictly logical inference, a world of order and law, of harmony and proportion, a world of system. These are postulates having chiefly an æsthetic warrant, rather than the warrant of strict logical inference from brute fact. They are none the less valid for all that. The fact is, that man is not merely logical intellect, but æsthetic life and feeling; and Truth and Reality reveal themselves to man not merely as intellectual, but also as æsthetical. And, as we distinguish the poet who deals with the problems of philosophy according to the usual methods of the philosopher from the poet who deals with them by intuition; so we may distinguish the poet-philosopher from the mere philosopher, not simply by the fact that the former records his reasoning and conclusions with respect to ultimate Truth and Reality in verse instead of prose, but also by the fact, that in his actual pursuit of knowledge the æsthetic life figures more conspicuously in his attainment of conclusions than it does in the case of the mere philosopher.

Now one of the most remarkable examples of actual philosophizing in verse is found in Sir John Davies's poem — *Nosce Teipsum*. A sixteenth-century production, to many students of literature and philosophy it belongs almost to the category of "half-forgotten lore." Indeed, it is questionable whether the poem is known at all to the large majority of students of philosophy.[1] However, it is worthy of a much better fate. Were an excuse needed for calling attention to this notable production, it could easily be found in the fact that, almost by common consent among competent literary critics, it is pronounced one of the best examples of philosophical poetry in our language. An excuse could be found also in the historical significance of the poem. That the first statement is correct will be apparent from an examination of the following record of critical opinion: —

Beginning with estimates of some of the earlier writers, Elizabeth Cooper, in her judgment of Davies, says: "[He] left behind Him more val-

---

[1] Of the many recognized histories of philosophy, the poem is mentioned by only one.

uable Witnesses of his Merit, than all the Titles that Heraldry can invent, or Monarchs bestow: The joint Applauses of *Cambden*, Sir *John Harington*, *Ben Johnson*, *Selden*, *Donn*, *Corbet*, &c.! These are great, and unquestionable Authorities in Favour of this Author; and I shall only presume to add, That, in my humble Opinion, no Philosophical Writer, I have met with, ever explain'd their Ideas more clearly, or familiarly even in Prose; or any so beautifully or harmoniously in Verse. There is a peculiar Happiness in his Similies, being introduc'd to illustrate, more than adorn; which renders them as useful, as entertaining; and distinguishes his from those of every other Author." [1]

In the next place, George Ellis, after referring to the fact that the *Theatrum Poetarum* contains the names of seventy-four poets belonging to the Elizabethan period, and to the further fact that most of them have been "consigned to oblivion," remarks, that "a few, such as Drayton, Fairfax, Warner, Sir John Harrington, Sir Philip Sidney, Sir Walter Raleigh, &c. continue to be cited in deference to their ancient reputation; but Shakspeare, Jonson, Fletcher, Spenser, and Sir John

[1] "The Muses' Library," 2d ed. London, Vol. I. p. 332.

Davies, are still confessed to be unrivalled in their several styles of composition, although near two centuries have elapsed, during which the progress of literature and the improvement of our language have been constant and uninterrupted." [1]   He further adds with respect to Davies: "His poem on the Immortality of the Soul is a noble monument of his learning, acuteness, command of language, and facility of versification. His similies (as Mrs. Cooper and Mr. Headley have justly observed) are singularly happy; always enlivening, and often illustrating his abstruse and difficult subject." [2]

More favorable still is the critical estimate of Hallam. He says: "Perhaps no language can produce a poem, extending to so great a length, of more condensation of thought, or in which fewer languid verses will be found. . . . Lines there are in Davies which far outweigh much of the descriptive and imaginative poetry of the last two centuries, whether we estimate them by the pleasure they impart to us, or by the intellectual vigour they display. Experience has

[1] "Specimens of the Early English Poets." London, 1811, Vol. II., pp. 157–158.

[2] Ibid., Vol. II. p. 369.

shown that the faculties peculiarly deemed poetical are frequently exhibited in a considerable
degree, but very few have been able to preserve
a perspicuous brevity without stiffness or pedantry
(allowance made for the subject and the times),
in metaphysical reasoning, so successfully as Sir
John Davies." [1]

Essentially the same view of Davies is taken
by Campbell, who says: "Davies's poem on
the Immortality of the Soul, entitled ' *Nosce teipsum*,' will convey a much more favourable idea
of metaphysical poetry than the wittiest effusions
of Donne and his followers. Davies carried abstract reasoning into verse with an acuteness and
felicity which have seldom been equalled. He
reasons, undoubtedly, with too much labour, for-
mality, and subtlety, to afford uniform poetical
pleasure. The generality of his stanzas exhibit
hard arguments interwoven with the pliant materials of fancy so closely, that we may compare
them to a texture of cloth and metallic threads,
which is cold and stiff, while it is splendidly
curious. There is this difference, however, between Davies and the commonly styled metaphys-

1 " Introduction to the Literature of Europe." London, 1839,
Vol. II. pp. 314-315.

ical poets, that *he* argues like a hard thinker, and *they*, for the most part, like madmen.   If we conquer the drier parts of Davies's poem, and bestow a little attention on thoughts which were meant, not to gratify the indolence, but to challenge the activity of the mind, we shall find in the entire essay fresh beauties at every perusal: for in the happier parts we come to logical truths so well illustrated by ingenious similes, that we know not whether to call the thoughts more poetically or philosophically just.   The judgment and fancy are reconciled, and the imagery of the poem seems to start more vividly from the surrounding shades of abstraction." [1]

Again, Professor Craik pays this high tribute to *Nosce Teipsum* and its author: "[The poem] is written in rhyme, in the common heroic ten-syllable verse, but disposed in quatrains, like the early play of Misogonus already mentioned, and other poetry of the same era, or like Sir Thomas Overbury's poem of The Wife, the Gondibert of Sir William Davenant, and the Annus Mirabilis of Dryden, at a later period.   No one of these writers has managed this difficult stanza so suc-

[1] "Essay on English Poetry," prefixed to "Specimens of the British Poets," 2d ed.   London, 1841, Pt. II. p. lxx.

cessfully as Davies: it has the disadvantage of
requiring the sense to be in general closed at
certain regularly and quickly recurring turns,
which yet are very ill adapted for an effective
pause; and even all the skill of Dryden has been
unable to free it from a certain air of monotony
and languor, — a circumstance of which that poet
may be supposed to have been himself sensible,
since he wholly abandoned it after one or two
early attempts. Davies, however, has conquered
its difficulties; and, as has been observed, 'perhaps no language can produce a poem, extending
to so great a length, of more condensation of
thought, or in which fewer languid verses will be
found.' [1] In fact, it is by this condensation and
sententious brevity, so carefully filed and elab-
orated, however, as to involve no sacrifice of
perspicuity or fulness of expression, that he has
attained his end. Every quatrain is a pointed
expression of a separate thought, like one of
Rochefoucault's Maxims; each thought being, by
great skill and painstaking in the packing, made
exactly to fit and to fill the same case." [2]

[1] Hallam, " Lit. of Europe," II. p. 227.
[2] "A Compendious History of English Literature." New York,
1863, Vol. I. p. 578.

An American critic, Edwin P. Whipple, speaks of Davies and his celebrated poem as follows: "It is usual among critics, even such critics as Hallam and Campbell, to decide that the imaginative power of the poem on the 'Immortality of the Soul' consists in the illustration of the arguments rather than in the perception of the premises. But the truth would seem to be that the author exhibits his imagination more in his insight than in his imagery. The poetic excellence of the work comes from the power of clear, steady beholding of spiritual facts with the spiritual eye, — of beholding them so clearly that the task of stating, illustrating, and reasoning from them is performed with masterly ease." [1]

George MacDonald also holds our poet's work in high esteem. Referring to *Nosce Teipsum*, he says: "It is a wonderful instance of what can be done for metaphysics in verse, and by means of imagination or poetic embodiment generally. . . . Sir John Davies's treatise is not only far more poetic in image and utterance than that of Lord Brooke, but is far more clear in argument and firm in expression as well." [2]

[1] "The Literature of the Age of Elizabeth." Boston, 1869, pp. 239–240.
[2] "England's Antiphon," pp. 105–106.

Grosart, the editor of Davies's works, says: "The nicety and daintiness of workmanship, the involute and nevertheless firmly-completed and manifested imagery of 'Nosce Teipsum' wherewith this nicety and daintiness are wrought, place Sir John Davies artistically among the finest of our Poets." [1] And again: "'Nosce Teipsum' as it was practically the earliest so it remains the most remarkable example of deep reflective-meditative thinking in verse in our language or in any language." [2]

Henry Morley, also, joins with the critics in praise of *Nosce Teipsum*. He says: " Its stanzas of elegiac verse were so well packed with thought, always neatly contained within the limit of each stanza, that we shall afterwards have to trace back to this poem the adoption of its measure as, for a time, our 'heroic stanza.'" [3]

Of similar character is the judgment of J. W. Hales: " In the kingdom of poetry, as has been said, are many mansions, and undoubtedly one of these belongs to Sir John Davies, however

[1] "The Complete Poems of Sir John Davies." London, 1876, Vol. I., Mem. Int. p. lxxxiii.

[2] Ibid., p. lx.

[3] " A First Sketch of English Literature." London, 1886, p. 459.

we may describe it, however we may censure its style and arrangement. Far be from us any such critical or scholastic formulæ as would prevent us from all due appreciation of such refined, imaginative thought and subtle, finished workmanship, as mark the first notable philosophical poem of our literature." [1]

Edmund Gosse also accords our author high praise. He says: " Sir John Davies, whose philosophical poems were among the most original and beautiful literary productions of the close of Elizabeth's reign, was suddenly silenced by the admiration James I. conceived for his judgment in practical affairs, and was henceforth wholly absorbed in politics. But an examination of Davies' work, had we space for it here, would form no ill preparation for the study of several classes of Jacobean poetry. He was eminently a writer before his time. His extremely ingenious *Orchestra*, a poem on dancing, has much in it that suggests the Fletchers on one side and Donne on the other, while his more celebrated *magnum opus* of the *Nosce Teipsum* is the general precursor of all the school of metaphysical ingenuity and argumentative imagination." [2]

[1] " Folia Litteraria," p. 163.
[2] " The Jacobean Poets." London, 1894, ch. i. pp. 8-9.

The number of these favorable critical estimates might easily be increased, but those given are enough, and sufficiently representative, to show that Davies is regarded by competent critical thought, not only as an artistic poet, but as one of the foremost writers of philosophy in verse in English poetry. This is no small merit, when we remember how largely poetry is dependent upon philosophy for her inspiration and content. It has been shown, by an appeal to the history of poetry, that the greatest poets have been those who have drunk from the cup of Philosophy. To think clearly on philosophical themes, and to present one's thinking in remarkably perfected verse, is a distinction that any poet might well covet. In the judgment of the critics this is a distinction which Davies undoubtedly possesses. In an elaborate poem, without diffuseness of thought or language, he proceeds carefully as a thinker and an artist, or rather as an artist-thinker, to work out a solution of some of the profoundest problems that can engage the human mind, and to present, in genuinely artistic form, not only the solution itself, but also the patient steps by which it was attained. A poet who undertakes conscientiously such a piece of work, and who suc-

cessfully accomplishes it, deserves well of every
student of literature and philosophy.

But, in the second place, Davies is by no means
unworthy of notice as a philosophic thinker. He
was possessed of the spirit of the true philosopher — of an earnest love for, and desire to know,
the truth. In his reasoning he is candid, and, for
the most part, free from dogmatism — especially
when viewed from the standpoint of the spirit of
his age. He stands ready all through the poem
to give a reason for the faith within him. He
does not underestimate the force of opposing
views, nor attempt to evade them. He meets
his antagonist fairly — whether he be sensational-
ist, materialist, sceptic, or Christian philosopher.
He does not proclaim merely, but philosophizes.
Furthermore, he reveals a strong grasp of the
problems of philosophy. This is not the case
with many of the philosophic poets, and there
is often a deficiency in this respect among philosophers themselves. Davies, throughout *Nosce
Teipsum*, seems to apprehend the essential nature
of the problems with which he deals. And to this,
as much as to anything, do we owe that clearness — that perspicacity — which his critics praise
so much. This is all the more evident, when we

note that he makes himself clearly understood in
verse — which does not lend itself so easily to
philosophical expression as prose. And it is still
more evident in view of the fact that he deals
with an exceedingly difficult stanza.

But after we have said all this, the real value
of his work as a philosopher lies in its historical
significance. Dr. Porter has truly stated what this
historical significance is. " It gives," he says, " a
transcript of that better scholastic doctrine of the
soul which combines the teachings of both Aristotle and Plato, when purified from many of the
extreme subtilities ingrafted upon them by the
doctors of the schools, and adds the results of
the dawning good sense which attended the Reformation and the Revival of Classical Learning.
For the history of philosophy it is of great significance, as it enables the student to understand
the psychology and philosophy which were current before the introduction of the philosophies
of Descartes on the one hand and of Hobbes and
Locke on the other." [1]

In somewhat similar vein Professor Morris remarks : " With considerable appositeness of argu-

[1] Ueberweg, " History of Philosophy," trans. by G. S. Morris.
New York, 1873, Vol. II., Appendix, pp. 352–353.

ment, and clearness of exposition, Sir John Davies sets forth his thoroughly spiritualistic psychology, and develops numerous considerations tending to establish the doctrine of the soul's immortality, all founded on the best philosophy the world had produced, and pervaded by an obvious breath of sincere and independent conviction. . . . The poem may stand as a document to prove what was the thoughtful faith of the best type of English gentlemen in his day." [1]

The historical significance of the poem as thus stated is not unimportant to the student of the history of psychology and philosophy. Works on the history of philosophy are not rich in materials to represent the period marking the transition from scholasticism to the birth of modern philosophy. So that any work, like Davies's *Nosce Teipsum*, which throws light on the best thought of this period, is of value to the student.

The work of a man, then, who is thus highly estimated as a poet and poet-philosopher by competent critics, and whose historical significance for students of psychology and philosophy is of such importance, is certainly worthy of careful study. And, as we note the progress of psychology and

[1] " British Thought and Thinkers."   Chicago, 1880, pp. 67–68.

philosophy since the poet's day, to the rewards of such a study will be added the additional recompense of which Goethe speaks in the following lines : —

" A great delight is granted
When, in the spirit of the ages planted,
We mark how, ere our time, a sage has thought,
And then, how far his work, and grandly, we have brought."
    Faust, Scene I. — Bayard Taylor's Translation.

CHAPTER I

BIOGRAPHICAL SKETCH. — RELATION TO THE AGE AND TO PRECEDING THOUGHT

WE can gain a clearer insight into Davies's philosophical poem by making a brief study of his life, and an inquiry into his relation to his age. His indebtedness to predecessors must also be considered.

Sir John Davies, poet, poet-philosopher, lawyer, and statesman, was born in Tisbury, Wiltshire, England, in 1569. He was the son of John Davies, of Chisgrove, also a lawyer, and country gentleman. His mother, Mary Bennett, was a member of a distinguished family. Davies "became a commoner of Queen's coll. about the beginning of Mich. term in the fifteenth year of his age, an. 1585, wherein having laid a considerable foundation of academical literature, partly by his own natural parts (which were excellent) and partly by the help of a good tutor, he was removed (having taken a degree in arts, as it seems) to the

Middle-Temple, wherein applying himself to the study of the common-law, tho' he had no great geny to it, was in fine (July 1595,) made a barrester." [1] There are evidences that, although Davies was an earnest student, he was nevertheless given to indulgence in the youthful extravagances more or less characteristic of the times. He associated with the wits and poets of the period, and the character of the epigrams penned by him at this time indicate that the moral tone of society was not very high. He was admitted to the bar, as has already been stated, in 1595. Two years earlier, his celebrated poem entitled *Orchestra, or a Poeme of Dauncing*, "was licensed to John Harison," although it seems not to have been published before 1596. This poem was dedicated to one Richard Martin, afterward Recorder of London, and a very dear friend of Davies. This fact is interesting in the light of subsequent events. Later a quarrel occurred between the two friends, the consequences of which completely changed the tenor of the poet's life. For some reason Davies took offence at Martin, who is represented as a man " fast of tongue and ribald of wit, with a

[1] Anthony-a-Wood, " Athenæ Oxonienses." London, 1815, Vol. II. p. 400.

dash of provocative sarcasm."[1] Davies resented
the offence by cudgelling him severely while dining
at the barrister's table in the Middle Temple.   On
account of this assault he was expelled from the
Bar.[2] His disbarment, however, was not, in the
end, a misfortune to him or to the world.   It, so
to speak, brought him to himself. Having been
thus humiliated, he returned to Oxford and re-
sumed his studies.   It proved to be a year of repentance and soul-searching — a year of serious
study and reflection — which resulted in a complete
reformation of life.   To this Davies himself testi-
fies in the following words descriptive of his own
experience : —

> " Yet if *Affliction* once her warres begin,
>   And threat the feebler *Sense* with sword and fire ;
>   The *Minde* contracts her selfe and shrinketh in,
>   And to her selfe she gladly doth retire :
>
> " As *Spiders* toucht, seek their webs inmost part;
>   As *bees* in stormes vnto their hiues returne ;
>   As bloud in danger gathers to the heart;
>   As men seek towns, when foes the country burn.
>
> " If ought can teach vs ought, *Afflictions* lookes,
>   (Making vs looke into our selues so neere,)
>   Teach vs to *know our selues* beyond all bookes,
>   Or all the learned Schooles that euer were.

[1] Grosart, op. cit., Mem. Int. p. xxii.
[2] For full account of the affair see Stowell, " Archæologia,"
Vol. XXI.

" This *mistresse* lately pluckt me by the eare,
  And many a golden lesson hath me taught;
  Hath made my *Senses* quicke, and Reason cleare,
  Reform'd my Will and rectifide my Thought.

" So doe the *winds* and *thunders* cleanse the ayre;
  So working lees settle and purge the wine;
  So lop't and prunèd trees doe flourish faire;
  So doth the fire the drossie gold refine.

" Neither *Minerua* nor the learnèd Muse,
  Nor rules of *Art*, nor *precepts* of the wise;
  Could in my braine those beames of skill infuse,
  As but the glance of this *Dame's* angry eyes.

" She within *lists* my ranging minde hath brought,
  That now beyond my selfe I list not goe;
  My selfe am *center* of my circling thought,
  Onely *my selfe* I studie, learne, and know."

But a moral reformation of Davies was not the
only outcome of this humiliation, with its consequent isolation and reflection. His self-contempla-
tion led to a serious study of the reality, nature,
origin, powers, dignity, and destiny of the human
soul, and the uses to which such a spiritual being
should be put; and to the embodiment of his reflections and conclusions in an elaborate poem
entitled *Nosce Teipsum*. In other words, *Nosce
Teipsum* — which is a philosophy of mind in verse
— was the fruit of his humiliation and repentance.

It is quite remarkable that a poem, representing
so much literary merit, and requiring so much
serious and sustained reflection, should have been
produced in less than a year, especially when it is
remembered that much of Davies's time was devoted to the earnest pursuit of his studies.   By the
persuasion, and through the kind offices, of Lord
Mountjoy, the poem was dedicated to Queen Elizabeth,[1] who was so greatly pleased with it that she
made him her servant in ordinary, and gave him
promises of promotion.   Of course, regardless of
the merits of the poem, the aged queen could not
have been altogether indifferent to the graceful
and flattering words of the dedicatory poem : —

" To that cleere maiestie which in the North
    Doth, like another Sunne in glory rise ;
    Which standeth fixt, yet spreads her heauenly worth ;
    Loadstone to hearts, and loadstarre to all eyes.

" Like Heau'n in all ; like th' Earth in this alone,
    That though great States by her support doe stand,
    Yet she herselfe supported is of none,
    But by the finger of the Almightie's hand :

[1] A MS. copy of the poem, dedicated to Ed. Cooke, Esq., a
friend of Davies, is preserved in Holkham Hall.   Another MS.
copy was dedicated to the Earl of Northumberland.   Cf. " Dictionary of National Biography," Vol. XIV. p. 141.

" To the diuinest and the richest minde,
    Both by Art's purchase and by Nature's dowre,
    That euer was from Heau'n to Earth confin'd,
    To shew the vtmost of a creature's power :

" To that great Spirit, which doth great kingdomes mooue,
    The sacred spring whence *right* and *honor* streames,
    Distilling *Vertue*, shedding *Peace* and *Loue*,
    In euery place, as *Cynthia* sheds her beames :

" I offer up some sparkles of that fire,
    Whereby wee *reason, liue, and moue,* and *be ;*
    These sparkes by nature euermore aspire,
    Which makes them to so *high* an *highnesse* flee.

" Faire *Soule,* since to the fairest body knit,
    You giue such liuely life, such quickning power,
    Such sweet celestiall influences to it,
    As keepes it still in youth's immortall flower :

" (As where the sunne is present all the yeere,
    And neuer doth retire his golden ray,
    Needs must the Spring bee euerlasting there,
    And euery season like the month of May.)

" O ! many, many yeeres may you remaine,
    A happy angell to this happy Land ;
    Long, long may you on Earth our empresse raigne,
    Ere you in Heauen a glorious angell stand.

" Stay long (sweet spirit) ere thou to Heauen depart,
    Which mak'st each place a heauen wherein thou art."

Nosce Teipsum, more than any other poem of its author, made a reputation for Davies. The same year of its publication came the *Hymnes of Astræa* — a series of hymns or short poems to Queen Elizabeth. There are twenty-six, flattering and fulsome, ascribing to her almost every human virtue. There is a hymn to her picture; one telling of her mind; others treating respectively " Of the Sun-beames of her Mind," " Of her Wit," " Of her Will," " Of her Memorie," " Of her Phantasie," " Of the Organs of her Minde," " Of the Passions of her Heart," " Of the Innumerable Vertues of her Minde," " Of her Wisdome," " Of her Justice," " Of her Magnanimitie," and " Of her Moderation."

Davies was now conspicuous in the public eye. He was on the high road to preferment. Other poets recognized his merit. He contributed *Minor Poems* to Davison's *Poetical Rhapsody.* Through the intercession of Lord Ellesmere, Keeper of the Great Seal, he was re-admitted to the Bar, having made the proper apologies. His apology to Martin led, at least, to a formal reconciliation of the former friends.[1] In 1601 he was made a member of Parliament for Corfe Castle.

[1] Cf. Grosart, op. cit., Mem. Int. pp. xxx–xxxi.

Martin was also in Parliament at this time. Davies was appointed a member of the " Grand Committee " to thank Queen Elizabeth for the withdrawal of certain patents which had led to great abuses. A new and corrected edition of *Nosce Teipsum* was issued in 1602. After the death of Queen Elizabeth in 1603, " he, with the Lord Hunsdon, went into Scotland to congratulate K. James as her lawful successor; and being introduced into his presence, the king enquired the names of those gentlemen who were in the company of the said lord, and he naming John Davies among, who stood behind, them, the king straitway asked, whether he was *Nosce Teipsum ?* and being answered that he was the same, he graciously embraced him, and thenceforth had so great a favour for him, that soon after [in 1603,] he made him his solicitor, and then his attorney-general in Ireland." [1] He distinguished himself in the important and difficult office of Solicitor General. His latest biographer gives him almost unmeasured praise for his work in behalf of Ireland and the Government.[2] In 1606 he was made Attorney General for Ireland. He was also appointed Sergeant-at-Arms. Davies

[1] Anthony-a-Wood, op. cit., Vol. II. p. 401.
[2] Grosart, op. cit., Mem. Int. pp. xxxv–xxxvii.

showed exceptional fitness for his work, and his
state papers evince a high order of legal ability
and statesmanship.   In 1607 he was knighted.

During his career in Ireland he was married to
Eleanor, youngest daughter of George, Lord Aud-
ley.   She was a singular woman, given to strange
prophecies and superstitions.   " What she usually
predicted," says Wood, " she folded up for the most
part in dark expressions, received from a voice,
which she frequently heard, as she used to tell her
daughter Lucy, and the others." [1]   She wrote *The
Stay of the Wise*, *The Restitution of the Reprobates*,
The Bride's Preparation, and *Tobit's Book*.   Two
children were born of the marriage.   One, an
idiotic son, died in his youth.   The other, Lucy
by name, grew up an exceedingly clever woman.
She married Ferdinand, Lord Hastings, later Earl
of Huntingdon.

To return to Davies, we find that he performed
his official duties in Ireland with exceptional thoroughness and ability.   He made a careful study
of the " Irish question," and in 1612 was published his admirable book, *A Discoverie of the
Trve Cavses why Ireland was neuer entirely Sub-
dued . . . vntill the Beginning of his Maiesties*

[1] Op. cit., p. 404.

happie Raigne. This same year saw him made King's Sergeant. He was also elected a Member of Parliament for Fermanagh, and later was chosen Speaker of the House. In 1614 he served as Member of Parliament for Newcastle-under-Lyne. Later, in 1619, he moved to England, continuing to represent Newcastle-under-Lyne in the House, and also serving in the capacity of Judge of Assize.[1] In 1622 he published for the first time a volume of his collected poems.[2] In 1626 he received the exalted honor of an appointment to the Lord Chief Justiceship. Unfortunately he did not live long enough to enter upon the duties of his office. On December 8 of the same year he died — it was supposed, according to Wood, of apoplexy. He was buried in St. Martin's Church, London. Shortly after, an elaborate inscription in Latin was placed on a pillar near his grave. Grosart's translation of this inscription, so far as it relates to his character and accomplishments, is as follows: " To God the Best and Greatest: Sacred. John Davys of knightly rank, having formerly discharged with prudence the highest duties of King's Attorney General in the realm of Ireland:

[1] Grosart, op. cit., Mem. Int. p. xliii–xlvii.

[2] For a list of Davies's prose works cf. Wood, op. cit.,Vol. II. pp. 402–403. Consult also Grosart's ed. of his collected prose works.

thence having been recalled to his own country,
secured the first place among the servants of his
lord the King, at the Law.   After various services
nobly rendered in each office, being now nom-
inated to more distinguished (appointments) he
suddenly frustrated the hope of his friends but
fulfilled his own — being called away from human
honours to celestial glory, in the year of his age
57.   A man for accomplished genius, for uncommon eloquence, for language whether free or
bound in verse, most happy.   Judicial sternness
with elegance of manners and more pleasant
learning he tempered.   An uncorrupt Judge, a
faithful Patron.   For love of free-born piety and
contempt for fretting superstition alike remarkable.   He looked down from on high on the
obstinate narrowness of plebeian souls in the
matter of religion, pity softening his disdain.
Himself magnanimously just, religious, free, and
moved by heaven." [1]

Davies, of course, like every writer, was affected
by the spirit of the age.   The spirit of the Elizabethan age has been so frequently portrayed,
and at such great length, in other works, as to
make an extended description here unnecessary.

[1] Op. cit., Mem. Int. pp. liv–lv.

A brief reference to it for purposes of understanding in what manner Davies in writing *Nosce Teipsum* was affected by it is all that is required.

The first results of the Revival of Letters were experienced by England in the latter part of the fifteenth and the first part of the sixteenth centuries. Probably the best results in the sixteenth century were reached during the reign of Henry VIII. But throughout the reign of Elizabeth there was considerable interest mauifested in classical literature. Professor Craik, in a chapter on "Classical Learning," [1] speaking of the sixteenth century, says: "The whole of the sixteenth century, however, will deserve the epithet of a learned age, notwithstanding the state of the schools and universities, and of what are called the learned professions, if we look either to the names of eminent scholars by which every portion of it is adorned, or to the extent to which the study of the learned languages then entered into the education of all persons, women as well as men, who were considered to be well educated." . . . "The number of very great English scholars, however, in the reign of Elizabeth was not so considerable as in that of her father, when

[1] Op. cit., Vol. I. p. 416 sq.

classical studies were not only cultivated with perhaps a truer appreciation of the highest models,
but afforded, besides, almost the only field for
intellectual exercise and display. Still this kind
of learning continued to be fashionable; and a
familiar, if not a profound, acquaintance with both
the Latin and the Greek languages was diffused
to an unusual extent among persons of the highest rank." [1] Elizabeth herself was a good Greek
scholar, and translated Isocrates. Ascham, in
the *Schoolmaster*, speaks well of her knowledge
of Latin. She translated a portion of Seneca's
Hercules Œtæus. The members of her court
were also interested in the classics. Warton,
speaking of Elizabeth's reign, says: " It became
fashionable in this reign to study Greek at court.
The maids of honour indulged their ideas of sen-
timental affection in the sublime contemplation of
Plato's Phædo: and the queen, who understood
Greek better than the canons of Windsor, and
was certainly a much greater pedant than her
successor James the First, translated Isocrates." [2]

Davies was undoubtedly affected by the literary

[1] Op. cit., Vol. I. pp. 428–429.

[2] "The History of English Poetry," etc. London, 1840, Vol.
III. p. 20.

spirit of the age. Classical training and learning figured in his education. Like other poets of the Elizabethan period, he reveals in his poetry a familiarity with Latin and Greek authors. There are numerous allusions to classical mythology in his writings. Not a few of these are to be found in *Nosce Teipsum*. They also indicate some knowledge of classical history. The acquaintance of our poet with classical literature naturally raises the question whether, since *Nosce Teipsum* is really the first formally developed system of philosophy in English poetry, its author found a model among the Greek or Latin poets. It has been suggested that he found such a model in the *De Rerum Natura* of Lucretius. However, there does not seem to be any substantial evidence for such a suggestion. External evidence on this point would only indicate a possibility of a knowledge of Lucretius as a result of Davies's interest in philosophy and classical literature. But internal evidence certainly does not indicate that the poem of Lucretius was the model for *Nosce Teipsum*. The two poems are altogether unlike, both in form and content. So far as form is concerned, their metrical framework is entirely different. So far as content is concerned, they differ radically. The work of Lucretius is much more comprehensive than is the work of Davies. The former is a philosophy of all reality — of things as well as of minds; the latter is merely a philosophy of mind. The former is a materialistic philosophy; the latter is a spiritualistic philosophy. Furthermore, the materialism which Davies refutes in *Nosce Teipsum*, which regards the soul as corporeal, is not peculiar to Lucretius, but is common to Democritus, the Stoics, and Epicureans as well. Again, in Davies's elaborate consideration of the objections to the immortality of the soul, he does not consider any of the many objections urged by Lucretius[1] against the belief. Even the idea of writing a philosophical poem does not seem to have been suggested by the work of Lucretius. The most natural explanation of the origin of *Nosce Teipsum* is the one already hinted at in the account given in the biographical sketch. Davies's disbarment, with the humiliation and disgrace involved, led him to betake himself to serious introspection and reflection. He himself tells us what the results of his "affliction" were: —

[1] "De Rerum Natura," Lib. III.

" If ought can teach vs ought, *Afflictions* lookes,
  (Making vs looke into our selues so neere,)
  Teach vs to *know our selues* beyond all bookes,
  Or all the learned Schooles that euer were.

" This *mistresse* lately pluckt me by the eare,
  And many a golden lesson hath me taught ;
  Hath made my *Senses* quicke, and Reason cleare,
  Reform'd my Will and rectifide my Thought.
  . . . .

" She within *lists* my ranging minde hath brought,
  That now beyond my selfe I list not goe ;
  My selfe am *center* of my circling thought,
  Onely *my selfe* I studie, learne, and know."

The conclusions born of such a soul-study Davies
desired to communicate to others; and, being a
poet, what more natural than that he should
choose verse as the means of communication?
The result was, a philosophical poem — *Nosce
Teipsum.*

But what of Davies's relation to the spirit of his
age so far as the philosophy and theology of his
poem are concerned? To what extent was he
influenced in his thinking by the philosophical and
theological thought of his time? This question
can best be answered in connection with a more
general question; namely, What are the chief
sources of Davies's philosophical indebtedness?
Philosophical thinkers generally are influenced by

their speculative environment and by preceding
speculative thought. Davies is no exception to
the rule. It is rather difficult to determine by
specific external evidence to whom he is specially
indebted. Internal evidence, however, seems to
point to the influence of four thinkers, — Aristotle,
Cicero, Nemesius, and Calvin.

In the first place, a careful comparison of Davies's
poem with Aristotle's *De Anima* reveals Davies's
acquaintance with this celebrated work of the great
Greek philosopher. This is manifest in the similarity of their teachings on fundamental points,
as, the reality of the soul, the nature of the soul,
the soul's relation to the body, the rational soul's
relation to sense, the powers of the soul, the activity of the soul, etc. These similarities of teaching
will be more specifically pointed out in the course
of our study, and they will be found sufficiently
striking to remove any scepticism concerning the
influence of the Stagyrite upon our poet's thinking. Of course external evidence would seem to
indicate this also. Aristotle was a power in Scholastic thought, and the Renaissance and Protestant
Reformation only led to a more *direct* study of
his works. Despite the early antipathy of the
theologians of the Reformation to Aristotle (as

for example Luther and Melancthon), later they found it necessary to turn to him for aid in their reconstruction of theology. But they turned to the real Aristotle rather than to his Scholastic interpreters. So that Aristotle was influential in the speculative thought of the sixteenth century. And it was quite natural that Davies should seek help from this powerful mind in his study of the human soul.

In the second place, internal evidence strongly indicates the influence of Cicero upon the thinking of Davies. This is manifest in his argument for the reality of the soul; but more especially in his argument for its immortality. The greater portion of his reasoning on this subject is taken from Cicero's *Tusculan Disputations.* The arguments from universal assent, from contempt of death in righteous souls, the fear of death in wicked souls, the intimations of immortality manifest in the desire for posthumous fame, and in the care for posterity; — all of this, as we shall see later by careful comparison, is taken from the Roman philosopher.

In the third place, internal evidence points more or less conclusively to the influence of Nemesius upon Davies. Nemesius was one of the early

Christian Fathers and Bishop of one of the cities
in Phœnicia.   He wrote a work in Greek on *The
Nature of Man*.   This work was translated into
English by George Wither, the poet, and published
in London, 1636.   In Nichols's *Literary Illustrations*[1] there is a letter written by one Alexander
Dalrymple to a Mr. Herbert in which, after stating
that he had recently purchased some old books,
he says: "I have also got 'Wither's translation
of Nemesius de Naturâ hominis' by which I
find Sir John Davies's poem on the Immortality
of the Soul is chiefly taken from Nemesius."
. . . "I have picked up a tract in 4to by Thomas
Jenner, with some very good plates, the marginal
notes of which seem to be what the heads of
Tate's edition of Sir John Davies's are taken
from."[2]

To Dalrymple's accusation of plagiarism on the
part of Davies Grosart takes vigorous exception.
He says: "Were this true it would utterly take
from 'Nosce Teipsum' the first characteristic and
merit I claim for it — deep and original thought.
But it is absolutely untrue, an utter delusion, as
any one will find who takes the pains that I have

---

[1] Vol. IV. pp. 549–550.
[2] Grosart, op. cit., Mem. Int. p. lxi.

done to read, either the original Nemesius, or what
this sapient book-buyer mentions, Wither's translation. With my mind and memory full of 'Nosce
Teipsum' and the poem itself beside me, I have
read and re-read every page, sentence and word of
Nemesius and Wither (and there is a good deal of
Wither in his translation: 1636) and I have not
come upon a single metaphor or (as the old margin-
notes called them) 'similies,' or even observation
in 'Nosce Teipsum' drawn from Nemesius or
Wither. The only element in common is that
necessarily Nemesius adduces and discusses the
opinions of the Heathen Philosophers on the many
matters handled by him, and Sir John Davies does
the same with equal inevitableness. But to base
a charge of plagiarism against 'Nosce Teipsum'
on this, is to reason on the connection between
Tenterden Steeple and Goodwin Sands (if the
well-worn folly be a permissible reference). . . .
Chronologically — Wither's translation was not
published until 1636, while 'Nosce Teipsum' was
published in 1599; but Nemesius' own book no
more than Wither's warrants any such preposterous
statements as this Alexander Dalrymple makes.
Even in the treatment of the 'opinions' of the
Heathen Philosophers which come up in Nemesius,

and in ' Nosce Teipsum,' the latter while ' inter-
medling' with the same returns wholly distinct
answers in refutation.   The ' opinions ' themselves
as being derived of necessity from the same
sources are identical; but neither their statement
nor refutation.   Nemesius is ingenious and well-
learned, but heavy and prosaic.   Sir John Davies
is light of touch and a light of poetic glory lies on
the lamest ' opinion.'   The ' Father of the Church '
goes forth to war with encumbering armour: the
Poet naked and unarmed beyond the spear wherewith he ' pierces ' everything, viz. human consciousness.   Jenner's forgotten book had perhaps been
read by Tate, but that concerns Tate not Sir John
Davies.   I pronounce it a hallucination to write
' Sir John Davies' poem on the immortality of the
Soul is chiefly taken from Nemesius.'   Not one
line was taken from Nemesius." [1]

As the view of Davies's indebtedness to Nemesius taken in this study differs materially from
the view of Grosart, it is only fair that his view
should be presented here in full.   Immediately
following the words quoted above, he proceeds
with equal vigor and firmness of conviction as
before : —

[1] Op. cit., Mem. Int. pp. lxi–lxiii.

"Before passing on it may be well to illustrate here from the 'contents' of two chapters (representative of the whole) in Wither's Nemesius, the merely superficial agreement between them and 'Nosce Teipsum.' In the Poem under 'The Soule of Man and The Immortalitie thereof' various opinions of its 'nature' are thus summarized:

'One thinks the *Soule* is *aire;* another, *fire;*
    Another *blood*, diffus'd about the heart;
    Another saith, the *elements* conspire,
    And to her *essence* each doth giue a part.

Musicians thinke our *Soules* are *harmonies*,
    Phisicians hold that they *complexions* bee;
    Epicures make them swarmes of *atomies*,
    Which doe by chance into our bodies flee.' (p. 26.)

In Nemesius, c. 2. § I, the 'headings' are: 'I. The severall and different Opinions of the Ancients concerning the Sovl, as whether it be a Substance; whether corporeall, or incorporeall, whether mortal or immortal. P. II. The confutation of those who affirme in general that the Sovl is a corporeall-substance. III. Confutations of their particular Arguments, who affirme that the Sovl is Blood, Water, or Aire.' These are all common-places of ancient 'opinion' and of the subject; and anything less poetical than Nemesius' treatment of them is

scarcely imaginable. Here if anywhere Davies'
indebtedness must have been revealed; but not
one scintilla of obligation suggests itself to the
Reader. Again in the Poem, after a subtle and
very remarkable 'confutation' of the notion that
the Soul is a thing of 'Sense' only, there comes
proof 'That the Soule is more than the Temperature of the humours of the Body'; and nowhere
does Davies show a more cunning hand than in
his statement of the 'false opinion.' Turning once
more to Nemesius c. II. § 3, these are its 'headings': — 'I. It is here declared, that the Soul is
not (as Galen implicitly affirmeth) a Temperature in
general. II. It is here proved also, that the Soul
is no particular temperature or quality. III. And
it is likewise demonstrated that the Soul is rather
governesse of the temperatures of the Body, both
ordering them, and subduing the vices which
arise from the bodily tempers.' Here again we
would have expected some resemblances or suggestions; but again there is not a jot or tittle of
either. Thus is it throughout. One might as well
turn up the words used in 'Nosce Teipsum' in a
quotation-illustrated Dictionary of the English Language (such as Richardson's) and argue 'plagiarism' because of necessarily agreeing definitions,

as from a few scattered places in ' Nosce Teipsum '
discussing the same topics, allege appropriation of
Nemesius. Your mere readers of title-pages and
contents, or glancers over indices are constantly
blundering after this fashion. Dalrymple was one
of these." [1]

Now, undoubtedly Dalrymple was in error in
accusing Davies of borrowing from Wither's translation of Nemesius's *De Natura Hominis*, for, as
Grosart points out, *Nosce Teipsum* was published
in 1599 and Wither's translation of Nemesius did
not appear in print until 1636. He was also in
error in making such a sweeping statement as " I
find Sir John Davies's poem on the Immortality
of the Soul is chiefly taken from Nemesius," for
the contents of the two volumes vary greatly. In
the first place, early in their works, both writers
treat of the Fall of Man, and they differ in their
conceptions of the consequences of the Fall.
Nemesius conceives of these as moral; whereas
Davies represents them as both moral and intellectual. In the second place, in his refutation of Materialism, Davies to a certain extent moves along
lines of argument differing from those of Nemesius. In the third place, in their discussions of the

[1] Op. cit., Mem. Int. pp. lxiii–lxvi.

reality of the soul, Davies presents an elaborate
refutation of Sensationalism, whereas Nemesius
is silent on this formidable theory.   In the fourth
place, Davies treats the question of the mode of
the Soul's origin in relation to the body much
more elaborately and after a different fashion than
does Nemesius.   They differ also in their conclusions on this question.   Davies is a Creationist,
whereas Nemesius believes in the doctrine of pre-
existence.   In the fifth place, there is a noticeable
difference in their psychological analysis — in their
analysis and division of mental powers or " faculties."   Davies presents a different classification,
and enumerates more " faculties " than does Nemesius.   In the sixth place, there is a difference in
their treatment of the subject of the soul's immortality.   The treatment of Nemesius, for a work of
such a character, is lamentably and inexcusably
meagre ; whereas Davies presents an elaborate discussion, involving numerous arguments for belief
in immortality, also objections and replies, as well
as misgivings and answers.   In all of these fundamental, as well as in many minor respects, the two
works differ so materially that an accusation of
plagiarism is utterly unjust.   Furthermore, Davies
reveals such great obligations to other thinkers as

to make an accusation of wholesale plagiarism from Nemesius, such as Dalrymple makes, absurd.

But while this may be said without fear of successful contradiction, a careful comparison of Davies's *Nosce Teipsum* with Nemesius's *De Natura Hominis* makes it impossible to agree with Grosart, that " Not one line was taken from Nemesius "; that "not one scintilla of obligation suggests itself to the Reader "; and that, with regard to " resemblances and suggestions," "there is not a jot or tittle of either." On the contrary, there are " resemblances and suggestions " of such a striking character as to indicate beyond reasonable doubt, that Davies was familiar with the Church Father's work, and was influenced by it to a considerable extent. These " resemblances and suggestions " will appear in our further study. They can hardly be accounted for on grounds of coincidence, or of dealing with the same question. They indicate rather, that Davies, like every intelligent author, in treating his subject, inquired into what his predecessors had said on the same subject; and that, in so doing, he found himself in accord with some of their views, and received valuable suggestions from them in forming still other views. They indicate, further, that Nemesius was one of the predecessors whom Davies had consulted with advantage.

Another thinker to whom our poet was indebted is Calvin. This is manifest in the more specifically theological portions of *Nosce Teipsum*, as in the discussion of the Fall of man in the first part of the poem; and the problem of original sin, in the second part. It was quite natural that, in seeking help on such subjects, he should turn to the works of a theologian whose influence was dominant in the Protestant theology of his country. A comparison of the theological portions of *Nosce Teipsum* with Calvin's *Institutes of the Christian Religion*, which will be made in the course of our interpretation of the poem, will indicate the extent of Davies's obligation to the Genevan theologian.

But although Davies was greatly indebted to these thinkers — Aristotle, Cicero, Nemesius, and Calvin — he reveals such a thorough grip on the problems of the philosophy of mind, and such a unique and clever way of dealing with them, as to make his philosophy and his philosophical poetry in a true sense *his own*.

CHAPTER II

OF HUMAN KNOWLEDGE

HAVING thus briefly studied the history of Davies and the sources of influence upon his thinking, let us next turn to a consideration of his philosophical poem. As has been suggested already, his most elaborate and important poem is *Nosce Teipsum*. This work is a unique production, presenting as it does, in a formal manner, a complete rational psychology or philosophy of mind in verse. It is, therefore, pre-eminently a didactic poem — the aim being to present systematically the author's speculations on the profound problems of the reality, nature, powers, and destiny of mind. The thought is not so much a means to an end as is the poetry. Poetry is used in the service of philosophy more than philosophy is used in the service of poetry. Light is to be thrown on great and vital problems, and poetry is used as the conduit of light.

4

The poem is divided into two parts — the first, dealing with human knowledge; the second, with the reality, nature, origin, powers, and immortality of the human soul. The first part serves as an introduction to the second. In it the poet takes an exceedingly discouraging view of human knowledge and of the mind's capacity to know. Knowledge is mixed with error and man's reason is dark. This fact admits of explanation. It was not always so. Once man possessed a God-infused knowledge, surpassing anything he has since acquired. Once Reason's eye was " sharpe and cleere," capable of approaching very near to the " Eternal Light." Thus it was in man's paradisiacal state. This was his intellectual status before the Fall. But the " Spirit of Lyes " suggested that he was blind because he knew not evil. The Devil could not show evil in the works of God while man stood in his perfection. If man was to know evil he must first do evil. This he did, and the result was fatal. Man " made Reason blind " " to give Passion eyes." Through these eyes he first saw the foul forms of misery and woe, of nakedness and shame. Reason grew dark and could no longer discern the fair forms of Good and Truth. An impaired intellectual and moral

vision was the outcome of man's fatal desire to
know : —

> " *Battes* they became, that *eagles* were before :
> And this they got by their *desire to learne.*"

And we are no better than they. We continue
to eat of the forbidden fruit. We continue to
indulge a desire to learn. We turn with vain
curiosity to find hidden knowledge in " bookes
prophane." And what, indeed, is this knowledge
we seek? It is a poor, vain, empty affair. What
is it —

> " but the sky-stolne fire,
> For which the *thiefe* still chain'd in ice doth sit?
> And which the poore rude *Satyre* did admire,
> And needs would kisse but burnt his lips with it.

> " What is it? but the cloud of emptie raine,
> Which when *Ioue's* guest imbrac't, hee monsters got?
> Or the false *payles* which oft being fild with paine,
> Receiv'd the water, but retain'd it not !

> " Shortly, what is it but the firie coach
> Which the *Youth* sought, and sought his death withal?
> Or the *boye's* wings, which when he did approch
> The *sunne's* hot beames, did melt and let him fall?"

Thus fruitless is our search for knowledge. After
perusing " all the learned Volumes," what can we
know or discern —

> " When *Error* chokes the windowes of the minde?"

What can we know when Reason's lamp which, before man's Fall, shone throughout his small world, like the sun in the sky, has become merely a half-extinct sparkle under ashes! How, under such conditions, can we recall the knowledge which was man's original possession by grace? A man painfully earning "a groate a day," might as well hope to replace the large patrimony wasted by a profligate father. The utter vanity of human efforts after knowledge is affirmed by those who have most profoundly considered man's capacity to know. They have found that with us —

> "Skill comes so slow, and life so fast doth flie,
> We learne so little and forget so much."

It was for this reason that the Greek philosopher said, —

> "'He knew nought, but that he nought did know.'"

And there was no mocking when "the great mocking-Master" said that "'Truth was buried deepe below.'" Furthermore, how can we expect to know *things*, when no one understands himself — his own soul? Why should we accept the judgments of the soul concerning *things*, when it is unable to give a judgment concerning itself — as to the how, whence, where, and what of its own existence? We seek to know all things without, but are strangers to that within which constitutes our real self. Why is this so? Is it because the mind is like the eye, which fails to see itself in seeing other things? No! For the mind, while being the knowing subject, can also be the object of its own knowledge. The real trouble lies in the *corruption* of the mind. " She is so corrupt, and so defac't," that she becomes frightened at her own image. Just as the fair lady in the fable, who was transformed into a cow because of her lust, became startled and fled in terror on beholding her changed self reflected in the stream, loathing " the watry glasse wherein she gaz'd," so it is with man's soul. Once she bore the image of God, being fair, and good, and pure. Now her beauties are marred by sin, and she —

" Doth of all sights her owne sight least endure."

This unsightliness of the soul leads her to turn away from herself, to seek delight in other things. And the prospect of external things is so inviting, so fair and agreeable, so sweet and alluring, that the mind succeeds in completely escaping from herself : —

" These things transport, and carry out the mind,
That with her selfe her selfe can neuer meet."

There is one thing, however, which brings the soul back to herself. It is affliction. Just as spiders seek the inmost part of their webs when touched; and bees return to their hives in case of storm; and the blood gathers to the heart when danger appears; and men seek the towns when foes burn the country, — so the mind leaves the things which are without, and returns to herself within, when affliction's wars begin. These menacings of affliction, which drive the mind back to herself, —

> " Teach vs to *know our selues* beyond all bookes,
>   Or all the learned Schooles that euer were."

Our poet, referring doubtless to the disgrace incident upon his quarrel with Martin, and his consequent disbarment, his self-isolation and reflection, informs us, that of late affliction had visited him and had taught him " many a golden lesson." It had quickened his senses, cleared his reason, reformed his will, and rectified his thought. It gave boundaries to his mind, so that it no longer ranged beyond itself: —

> " My selfe am *center* of my circling thought,
>   Only *my selfe* I studie, learne, and know."

The results of this introspection and reflection are presented in the second part of the poem, entitled, *Of the Soule of Man and the Immortalite thereof.*

———————

Before entering upon a study of this second part of the poem it may be well to observe that the theory of knowledge contained in the poet's Introduction is not peculiar to Davies. In teaching an intellectual as well as a moral Fall of man he was simply expressing a view which was in accord with the prevalent Protestant theology of his time. It is the view of the Fall taught by Calvin in the *Institutes of the Christian Religion*, and attributed by him to Augustine. In his celebrated work just mentioned Calvin says: " I feel pleased with the well-known saying which has been borrowed from the writings of Augustine, that man's natural gifts were corrupted by sin, and his supernatural gifts withdrawn; meaning by supernatural gifts the light of faith and righteousness, which would have been sufficient for the attainment of heavenly life and everlasting felicity. Man, when he withdrew his allegiance to God, was deprived of the spiritual gifts by which he had been raised to the hope of eternal salvation. Hence it follows, that he is now an exile from the kingdom of God, so that all things which pertain to the blessed life of

the soul are extinguished in him until he recover
them by the grace of regeneration.   Among these
are faith, love to God, charity towards our neighbour, the study of righteousness and holiness.   All
these, when restored to us by Christ, are to be
regarded as adventitious and above nature.   If so,
we infer that they were previously abolished.   On
the other hand, soundness of mind and integrity
of heart were, at the same time, withdrawn, and it
is this which constitutes the corruption of natural
gifts.   For although there is still some residue of
intelligence and judgment as well as will, we cannot call a mind sound and entire which is both
weak and immersed in darkness.   As to the will,
its depravity is but too well known.   Therefore,
since reason, by which man discerns between good
and evil, and by which he understands and judges,
is a natural gift, it could not be entirely destroyed;
but being partly weakened and partly corrupted,
a shapeless ruin is all that remains.   In this sense
it is said, (John i. 5), that ' the light shineth in
darkness, and the darkness comprehended it not';
these words clearly expressing both points, viz.,
that in the perverted and degenerate nature of
man there are still some sparks which show that
he is a rational animal, and differs from the brutes,

inasmuch as he is endued with intelligence, and yet, that this light is so smothered by clouds of darkness that it cannot shine forth to any good effect. In like manner, the will, because inseparable from the nature of man, did not perish, but was so enslaved by depraved lusts as to be incapable of one righteous desire." [1]

The cumulative evidence of Davies's indebtedness to Calvin is such that it seems probable that he derived his conception of an intellectual Fall (which, as an *explicit* doctrine, is by no means common in Christian Theology) from him. Both thinkers are in agreement in regard to man's moral and intellectual status before the Fall. Man was then morally pure, and possessed of great intellectual strength. Of man's mental power prior to the Fall Calvin says: "Man excelled in these noble endowments in his primitive condition, when reason, intelligence, prudence, and judgment, not only sufficed for the government of his earthly life, but also enabled him to rise up to God and eternal happiness." [2]

To the same effect, and in similar language,

---

[1] "Institutes of the Christian Religion," trans. by Henry Beveridge. Edinburgh, 1845, Vol. I. Bk. II. ch. ii. sec. 12. All quotations from Calvin are from Beveridge's translation.

[2] Op. cit., Vol. I. Bk. I. ch. xv. sec. 8.

Davies describes the intellectual power of man
before the Fall : —

> " And when their reason's eye was sharpe and cleere,
>   And (as an eagle can behold the sunne)
>   Could haue approcht th' Eternall Light as neere,
>   As the intellectuall angels could haue done," etc.

Furthermore, both writers affirm a great intellectual and moral corruption and decline to be
the consequence of the Fall.   Here again, in the
statement of the consequences to man's intellectual
nature, there is not only sameness of teaching but
similarity of language.   Calvin, as we have seen
in the quotation above, says : " Reason, by which
man discerns between good and evil, and by which
he understands and judges," became weak and
corrupt, and his previously sound mind became
" immersed in darkness."   So Davies affirms : —

> " But then grew *Reason* darke, that *she* no more,
>   Could the faire formes of *Good* and *Truth* discern;
>   *Battes* they became, that *eagles* were before:
>   And this they got by their *desire to learne.*"

Again, they use similar language in describing
more specifically the modicum of intelligence left
to man after the Fall.   Calvin says, as we have
seen above, that man has still some " sparks " of
intelligence left; but " that this light is so smoth-

ered by clouds of darkness that it cannot shine
forth to any good effect."

Davies likewise affirms, that " Reason's lampe " —

" Is now become a sparkle, which doth lie
  Vnder the ashes, halfe extinct, and dead."

And, he asks : —

" How can we hope, that through the eye and eare,
  This dying sparkle, in this cloudy place,
  Can recollect these beames of knowledge cleere,
  Which were infus'd in the first minds by grace ? "

So that we find not only a sameness of doctrine
here but also a striking similarity of language in
which the doctrine is presented.

Furthermore, Calvin in this same chapter (Bk. II.
ch. ii.), which deals with the Fall of man, evaluates
human knowledge just as Davies does in this connection in the verses quoted above. Both pronounce severely on its emptiness and vanity. He
says: "There is, therefore, now, in the human
mind, discernment to this extent, that it is naturally influenced by the love of truth, the neglect of
which in the lower animals is a proof of their gross
and irrational nature. Still it is true that this love
of truth fails before it reaches the goal, forthwith
falling away into vanity. As the human mind is

unable, from dulness, to pursue the right path of investigation, and, after various wanderings, stumbling every now and then like one groping in darkness, at length gets completely bewildered, so its whole procedure proves how unfit it is to search the truth and find it." [1]

It is just in this vein that the poet speaks of the vanity of human knowledge when he describes it as the " sky-stolne fire " by kissing which the admiring Satyr burned his lips; and as " the cloud of emptie raine " which, when embraced by Jove's guest, yielded only monsters; and as false pails, which, being filled by painful labor, failed to retain the water; and as the fiery coach, the seeking of which brought death to the youth; and, finally, as the boy's wings, which, as he approached the sun, melted " and let him fall."

Thus early, then, in the poem, do we find, in the similarity of thought and language, evidence of the influence of Calvin on the poet. Further study of the poem will make this influence more manifest.

After Calvin's time the doctrine of an intellectual Fall was affirmed by the Synod of Dort, in the following words: —

[1] Op. cit., Vol. I. Bk. II. ch. ii. sec. 12.

"Homo ab initio ad imaginem DEI conditus vera et salutari sui Creatoris et rerum spiritualium notitia in mente, et justitia in voluntate et corde, puritate in omnibus affectibus exornatus, adeoque totus sanctus fuit; sed Diaboli instinctu, et libera sua voluntate a Deo desciscens, eximiis istis donis seipsum orbavit: atque e contrario eorum loco coecitatem, horribiles tenebras, vanitatem, ac perversitatem judicii in mente, malitiam, rebellionem, ac duritiem in voluntate et corde, impuritatem denique in omnibus affectibus contraxit." [1]

The same doctrine is affirmed by the Reformed Dutch Church in America, it being an adoption from the Canons of the Synod of Dort: " Man was originally formed after the image of God. His understanding was adorned with a true and saving knowledge of his Creator, and of spiritual things; his heart and will were upright; all his affections pure, and the whole Man was holy; but revolting from God by the instigation of the devil, and abusing the freedom of his own will, he forfeited these excellent gifts, and on the contrary entailed on himself blindness of mind, horrible darkness, vanity, and perverseness of judgment; because wicked,

---

[1] Canones Synodi Dordrechtanæ, 1618–1619, Tertium et Quartum Doctrinæ Caput, Art. Primus.

rebellious, and obdurate in heart and will, and impure in (all) his affections."[1]

The doctrine of an intellectual Fall appears also in recent theology. It is involved in the epistemology underlying the theology of some modern German theologians, one of the cardinal features of which is, that man's capacity to know the truth is materially affected by his moral character. Which conception, as applied to the doctrine of the Fall, would imply at least this much, that whatever may have been man's intellectual capacity prior to the Fall, the Fall being a moral one, necessarily involved an intellectual Fall as well. With Davies the intellectual power of man in the paradisiacal state was exceedingly great. He was an intellectual giant. Reason, as we have seen, was "sharpe and cleere," with a capacity of approaching very near to the "Eternal Light." His intellectual Fall was correspondingly great. It was a serious darkening of the moral and mental vision. And this moral impotency has been entailed upon the race. Hence the disparaging view, taken by our poet, of human knowledge and man's capacity to know.

[1] "Constitution of the Reformed Church in America." Cf. Schaff, "The Creeds of Christendom." New York, 1877, pp. 587–588.

CHAPTER III

MEANS BY WHICH THE SOUL IS KNOWN

IF we turn now to the second part of *Nosce
Teipsum* we are brought into contact with the
real subject-matter of the poem.   It is here that
the poet first really begins to philosophize.   We
find here a formal development in verse of a complete philosophy of mind.   This second part of
the work opens with a statement of the means by
which knowledge of the human soul is to be attained.   It is not by the eye of sense, he tells us,
that a knowledge of the soul is to be gained.
Sense deals with external objects.   It must, therefore, be by the aid of some other method.   God
has infused in man " an inward light " by which
his soul can gain a vision of herself.   The soul,
although endowed with the power of reflection,
needs divine aid to see herself aright.   The poet,
undertaking the study of his soul, realizes all the
more keenly his helplessness without divine aid, in

view of the ignorance of great minds concerning the essential nature and location of the soul. For, as he points out, —

> " One thinks the *Soule* is *aire ;* another, *fire ;*
> Another *blood*, diffus'd about the heart ;
> Another saith, the *elements* conspire,
> And to her *essence* each doth giue a part.

> " *Musicians* thinke our *Soules* are *harmonies*,
> *Phisicians* hold that they *complexions* bee ;
> *Epicures* make them swarmes of *atomies*,
> Which doe by chance into our bodies flee.

> " Some thinke one generall *Soule* fils euery braine,
> As the bright *sunne* sheds light in euery starre ;
> And others thinke the name of *Soule* is vaine,
> And that we onely *well-mixt* bodies are.

> " In judgement of her *substance* thus they vary ;
> And thus they vary in iudgement of her *seat ;*
> For some her chaire vp to the braine doe carry,
> Some thrust it downe into the *stomackes* heat.

> " Some place it in the root of life, the *heart ;*
> Some in the *liuer*, fountaine of the veines ;
> Some say, *Shee is all in all, and all in part :*
> Some say, She is not contain'd but all containes.

> " Thus these great clerks their little wisdome show,
> While with their doctrines they at *hazard* play,
> Tossing their light opinions to and fro,
> To mock the *lewd*, as learn'd in this as they.

" For no craz'd braine could euer yet propound,
   Touching the *Soule*, so vaine and fond a thought,
   But some among these masters haue been found,
   Which in their *Schooles* the self-same thing haue taught."

This diversity of human opinion and confusion of thought concerning the nature and location of the soul Davies regards as God's punishment for pride of intellect. God, alone, who knows the nature and powers of the soul, can help man to this knowledge. And the poet thinks that this divine aid has come to him, so that now he can understand the soul in her essential constitution. He thinks that, by the light of the " clear lampe " of God's " Oracle diuine," he is now able to trace the subtle lines of the soul's immortal face.

In the above statement of means by which knowledge of the soul is to be attained the poet still seems to be under the influence of an epistemology born of theological belief. The necessity of Divine aid in seeking a knowledge of God and the soul is a characteristic doctrine of Christian theology. Calvin affirms it as an essential condition of our knowledge of God and our relations to Him.[1] This may be another instance of the influence of the

[1] Op. cit., Bk. II. ch. ii. secs. 18, 19, sq.

theologian upon the poet-philosopher. However, while this is doubtless true, there is much truth also in the words of Professor Morris: " But guard against supposing that Sir John Davies could be led to assert the indispensableness of this light only out of deference, or from blind subjection, to the dictum of a revealed or currently established theology. Christian philosophy does indeed assert this, but, not only Christian philosophy, all systems of affirmative (not negative, empirical, " subjective ") Idealism, be they called after the names of Plato or Aristotle, of Descartes, Spinoza or Leibnitz, of Berkeley, Kant or Hegel, also assert, in some form, and of necessity, the same thing. The very sense of philosophical Idealism is to put and represent man in direct relation with the Absolute Mind, so that his light is its light, and its strength is made his." [1]

It was noted above that Davies felt the necessity of divine aid in his study of the human soul all the more because of the confusion of thought which reigned among " the great wits " on this subject: —

> " For her true forme how can my sparke discerne ?
> Which dim by *nature*, *Art* did neuer cleare ;
> When the great wits, of whom all skill we learn,
> Are ignorant both *what* shee is, and *where*."

[1] Op. cit., p. 65.

And then he illustrates this confusion of thought by citing numerous examples. Aristotle, in the beginning of the *De Anima,* also calls attention to the variety of speculative opinions in regard to the soul.[1] So, also, do Cicero,[2] and Nemesius.[3] Taken together, they refer to essentially the same set of opinions as to the nature of the soul found in Davies's list of references. Davies, however, simply cites the opinions and does not give the names of their authors. A comparison of their statements will leave no doubt as to the sources of Davies's information on these subjects. It will also acquaint us with the ultimate sources of these speculative views.

The first opinion of the soul which the poet cites is, that the soul is air. " One thinks the *Soule* is *aire.*" Aristotle says : " Diogenes as also some others resolved soul into air, supposing that this was the subtlest of all things and, at the same time, a principle of existence." [4] Cicero refers to this view as a common opinion.[5] Nemesius refutes the doctrine of the soul as air.[6]

---

[1] Bk. I. ch. ii.

[2] " Disputationes Tusculanæ," Lib. I. §§ 9–11.

[3] Op. cit., ch. ii. sec. 1.

[4] " De Anima," Bk. I. ch. ii. sec. 15. All quotations are from Wallace's translation.

[5] Op. cit., Bk. I. secs. 9–11.

[6] Op. cit., p. 94. All quotations are from Wither's translation.

The next opinion referred to is, that the soul is fire.

"One thinks the *Soule* is *aire*; another, *fire*."

Aristotle says: "Democritus, whose view agrees with that of Leucippus, consequently maintained soul to be a sort of fire and heat."[1]   Again, "Heraclitus also identifies the soul with his principle in describing it as the 'fiery process' out of which he derives other existing things, his ground being that it is that which is least corporeal and in constant movement."[2]   Cicero says: "The soul seems to Zeno the Stoic to be fire."[3]   Nemesius attributes this conception of the soul as fire to the Stoics. "The *Stoicks* affirm, that it is a certain *Blast, hot and fiery*."[4]

The third view of the nature of the soul referred to by Davies is, that it is blood: —

"Another *blood*, diffus'd about the heart.

Aristotle says: "Others again, like Critias, have identified the soul with blood, regarding sentiency as the most distinctive characteristic of the soul

[1] Op. cit., Bk. I. ch. ii. sec. 3.

[2] Ibid., Bk. I. ch. ii. sec. 16.

[3] Op. cit., Bk. I. sec. 9. All quotations from Cicero are from Yonge's translation. New York, 1877.

[4] Op. cit., p. 78.

and viewing this sentient capacity as due to the
element of blood." [1]   Cicero says: " Empedocles
imagines the blood, which is suffused over the
heart, to be the soul." [2]   So Nemesius, " *Critias*
holds, that it is *bloud*." [3]

The next view cited by Davies is, that the soul
is composed of the four elements: —

> "Another saith, the *elements* conspire
> And to her *essence* each doth giue a part."

Aristotle says: " Thus Empedocles makes the
soul to be composed of all the elements, and at
the same time considers each one of these elements a soul.   His words are as follows:

> ' Surely by earth we perceive earth, and man knoweth water
> by water.
> By air sees air the divine ; by fire sees fire the destructive:
> Yea, love comprehends love, and 'tis through strife dismal
> we know strife.'

In this same fashion also does Plato in the Timæus construct the soul out of the elements." [4]

Again Davies says: —

> " *Musicians* thinke our *Soules* are *harmonies*."

[1] Op. cit., Bk. I. ch. ii. sec. 19.
[2] Op. cit., Bk. I. sec. 9.
[3] Op. cit., p. 78.
[4] Op. cit., Bk. I. ch. ii. secs. 6, 7.

Cicero says: "There were many among the ancients who held singular opinions on this subject,
of whom the latest was Aristoxenus, a man who
was both a musician and a philosopher. He maintained a certain straining of the body, like what is
called harmony in music, to be the soul, and believed that, from the figure and nature of the whole
body, various motions are excited, as sounds are
from an instrument. He adhered steadily to his
system, and yet he said something, the nature of
which, whatever it was, had been detailed and
explained a great while before by Plato." [1] Nemesius refers to this view in the words: " And,
because *Dinarchus* defines the *Soul* to be an
Harmonie; [i. e. of the four elements]; and *Sim-
mias*, contradicting *Socrates*, affirms the same;
comparing the *Soul* to an *harmonie*, and the body
to a *Harp;* we will here set downe the same confutations of them, which we find in *Plato's* Dia-
logue called *Phædo*." [2]

Again, Davies says: —

> " *Phisicians* hold that they *complexions* bee."

Davies refers here, doubtless, to the view of the
soul which he takes pains later to refute; namely,

---

[1] Op. cit., Bk. I. sec. 10.
[2] Op. cit., p. 108.   Not " Dinarchus," but Dicæarchus.

the view which identifies the soul with the well-
tempered humors of the body — or " the temperature of the body." The word " complexions " is
thus used by Nemesius. He says: " Some will
aske, perhaps, how it comes to passe, (*if the soule
be not the temperature of the body*) that men are
vitious or vertuous, according to their naturall *con-
stitutions* and *complexions :* " [1] etc. The view of
the soul thus spoken of by Davies is attributed
by Nemesius to the physician Galen. He says:
" *Galen*, hath determined nothing peremptorily of
the SOUL; yea, hee himselfe affirmeth plainly, in
his writings of *demonstration*, that hee hath deliv-
ered nothing precisely of the same : But, it may
be collected by some of his expressions, that he
could be best pleased to affirm that the SOUL is a
temperature." [2]

Next, Davies refers to the Epicurean view of the
soul : —

> " *Epicures* make them swarmes of *atomies*,
> Which doe by chance into our bodies flee."

Of course, as Aristotle antedates Epicurus, there is
no reference in the *De Anima* to his view. But
we find there a reference to the atomic theory of
the soul. Such an atomic conception is involved

---

[1] Op. cit., p. 123.　　　[2] Op. cit., pp. 114–115.

in the views of Democritus and Leucippus already referred to. The spherical atoms according to these thinkers constitute fire. And, says Aristotle, " The reason why they maintain that the spherical atoms constitute the soul, is that atoms of such configuration are best able to penetrate through everything, and to set the other things in motion at the same time as they are moved themselves, the assumption here being that the soul is that which supplies animals with motion."[1] Cicero refers to the atomic theory of Democritus.[2] Nemesius refers to Epicurus's view of the Soul in connection with Democritus and the Stoics, refuting them as Materialists — regarding the soul as " body." He refers to the atomism of Democritus only.[3]

Davies next refers to the doctrine of a universal soul. He says : —

> " Some thinke one generall *Soule* fils euery braine,
>   As the bright *sunne* sheds light in euery starre."

Davies may refer here to Plato's doctrine of the " world-soul," which he develops in the *Phædrus,* *Timæus*, *Philebus*, and the *Laws*. Or, his reference may be to the doctrine mentioned by Neme-

---

[1] Op. cit., Bk. I. ch. ii. sec. 3.
[2] Op. cit., Bk. I. sec. 11.   [3] Op. cit., pp. 78–79.

sius: " Besides all these, some were of opinion
that there was but *one* and the *same* SOUL belonging to all things; which was by smal portions distributed to all particular things; and, then
gathered into it self againe: of which opinion were
the *Manichees* and certain others." [1] This was
also a Stoic conception.

Davies continues: —

> " And others thinke the name of *Soule* is vaine,
> And that we onely well-mixt bodies are."

According to Cicero, Pherecrates held there is no
such thing as a soul, "but that it is a name without a meaning; and that it is idle to use the expressions 'animals,' or 'animated beings'; that
neither men nor beasts have minds or souls, but
that all that power by which we act or perceive is
equally infused into every living creature, and is
inseparable from the body, for if it were not, it
would be nothing; nor is there anything whatever
really existing except body." [2]

From this difference of opinion in regard to the
substance of the soul, Davies turns to a similar difference of opinion in regard to the "seat" or location of the soul. Neither Aristotle nor Nemesius

---

[1] Op. cit., pp. 81–82.   [2] Op. cit., Bk. I. sec. 10.

discusses the opinions of " the great wits" on this subject, although they discuss at length the relation of the soul to the body. The opinions to which Davies refers are, first, the localizing of the soul in the brain : —

> " In iudgement of her *substance* thus they vary ;
> And thus they vary in iudgement of her *seat;*
> For some her chaire vp to the braine doe carry."

The Pythagoreans divide the soul into three parts, Reason, Mind, and Courage, localizing Reason and Mind in the brain, and Courage in the heart.[1] Plato took the tripartite view of the soul — regarding Reason or the rational part of the soul as localized in the head.   In that singular account of the formation of man contained in the *Timæus* he says: "That which, like a field, was to receive the divine seed, he made round every way, and called that portion of the marrow, brain, intending that, when an animal is perfected, the vessel containing this substance should be the head; but as touching the remaining and mortal part of the soul — that which was intended to contain this — he divided into round and long figures, and he called them all by the name ' marrow'; and from these, as

[1] Cf. Zeller, " Pre-Socratic Philosophy," trans. by S. F. Alleyne, Vol. I. pp. 480–481.

from anchors, casting the bonds of the whole soul, he proceeded to fashion around them the entire framework or our body, constructing for the marrow, first of all, a complete covering of bones." [1] Strato of Lampsacus also localized the soul in the head.[2] This, also, was the view of those writers in the Middle Ages who identified the soul with the animal spirits which were supposed to be the result of transforming the vital spirits in the brain, a more specific account of which will be given later. Davies himself regarded the brain as the " seat " of the soul: —

" This Lampe through all the regions of my braine,
Where my *soule* sits, doth spread such beames of grace."

And again: —

" Right so the *Soule*, which is a lady free,
    And doth the iustice of her *State* maintaine;
    Because the senses ready seruants be,
    Attending nigh about her Court, the braine."

The next view of the location of the soul to which Davies refers is, that: —

" Some thrust it downe into the *stomackes* heat."

[1] *Timæus*, 73, Jowett's trans. Cf. also Cicero, op. cit., Bk. I. sec. 10.
[2] Zeller, " Outlines of the History of Greek Philosophy," trans., p. 225.

This view has been attributed to the Pythagoreans. But, as seen above, they held an entirely different conception.

Again, speaking of still another view on this subject, he says : —

"Some place it in the root of life, the *heart*."

This view of the "seat" of the soul was quite common among the Stoics. "This fire of the soul is nourished by the blood, and the governing part of the soul (the ἡγεμονικόν) has its seat in the heart, the centre of the course of the blood (according to Zeno, Cleanthes, Chrysippus, &c., from whom only a few authors deviate)." [1] This was also a common conception among the Hebrews.

Another view referred to by Davies is, that some locate the soul in the liver : —

"Some in the *liuer*, fountaine of the veines."

Plato locates a "portion" of the soul "about" the liver which he makes the source of "prophetic intimations." Speaking of the liver, he says: "And the converse happens when some gentle inspiration of the understanding pictures images of an opposite character, and allays the bile and bitterness by not stirring them, and refuses to

[1] Zeller, op. cit., p. 244.

touch the nature opposed to itself, but by making use of the natural sweetness of the liver,
straightens all things and makes them to be right
and smooth and free, and makes the portion
of the soul which resides about the liver happy
and joyful, having in the night a time of peace
and moderation, and the power of divination in
sleep when it no longer participates in sense and
reason." [1]

And, finally, Davies says: —

> " Some say, *Shee is all in all, and all in part :*
> Some say, She is not contaerd but all containes."

He probably refers to the views of Nemesius
which embody all that is expressed in these
words. Speaking of the relation of soul to body
the Church Father says: " For, as the *Sun*, so
soon as it appeareth, changes the *ayre* into *light ;*
so making it lightsome, and so diffusing it selfe
with the *ayre*, that it is united with the same, and

---

[1] *Timæus*, 71, Jowett's trans. Referring to the Semitic conception, Kennedy says: " This peculiar sanctity of the visceral
fat, is to be explained by the fact that the liver and kidneys, with
the fat surrounding them, were regarded by the Semitic races as
being with the blood, the seat of life. . . ."

" Like the kidneys, the liver was also regarded as an important
seat of emotion." — Hastings, " A Dictionary of the Bible." New
York, 1900, p. 128.

yet not confounded therewith: Even so, the *soul*
being united with the *Body*, remains without confusion therewith; differing in this onely, that the
Sunne being a *Body*, and circumscribed within the
compasse of *Place*, is not himselfe in every place
where his *light* is, but (as *fire* in the *wood*, or as
the *flame* in a *candle*) is confined to a certaine
place.

"It is not so with the *soul*.   For, being void of
all *Body*, and not contained within the limits of any
place, it passeth *all* and *whole*, through its own
whole *light*, and through the whole *Body*, wherein
it is; neither is any part of it illuminated thereby,
wherein it is not fully and wholly present.   Neither
is it in the *body* as in some bottle or other vessell,
nor compassed in by the same; but the *Body* is
rather in the *soule*, and is thereby held in and
fastned together."[1]   Here we have the doctrine
of the soul being "all in all, and all in part"; and
that "she is not contain'd but all contains."
As will be seen later, this is the view of Davies
also.

This variety of opinion, then, in regard to the
"what" and "where" of the soul indicated to
Davies's mind the ignorance of "the great wits"

[1] Op. cit., pp. 197–199.

on these subjects. And this confusion " among
men's wits " was God's punishment for " pride of
wit." And, if such great minds, " of whom all
skill we learn," were unable to throw light on these
great questions of the soul, Davies felt that his
own mind, —

> "Which dimme by *nature*, *Art* did neuer cleare";

would certainly be insufficient for such knowledge,
unless aided by Divine light. Hence the prayer : —

> " *O Light* which mak'st the light, which makes the day !
> Which setst the eye without, and mind within ;
> 'Lighten my spirit with one cleare heauenly ray,
> Which now to view it selfe doth first begin."

CHAPTER IV

REALITY OF THE SOUL. — SENSATIONALISM

HAVING thus explained by what means the soul is to be known, Davies proceeds to unfold to us his philosophy of mind. The first problem with which he deals is the *reality* of mind.

The mind, according to our poet, is a reality — a real substance and spirit. Though united to the body, which serves as an apt means for the exercise of her powers, she is nevertheless, so far as her essential being is concerned, independent of the body. This reality of the soul is affirmed also in its relation to sense. The soul is not merely a derivative of sense. Its essential being consists not in sense, but in higher powers. The senses are merely the servants of the soul. They are mere attendants at her court — the brain. Now this self-being of the soul, which in a manner is independent of the body and the senses, is greatly emphasized by Davies. He insists upon it very early in the second part of his poem, and maintains it at length in an elaborate argument against two prominent types of Philosophy — Sensationalism and Materialism. The theory of Sensationalism, which explains all of the higher activities of mind, such as memory, imagination, conception, judgment, reasoning, will, etc., and, indeed, the very mind itself, on the basis of sensations and their mechanical groupings, is such a formidable theory, involving such serious consequences, that the poet enters upon an elaborate consideration of it, earnestly attempting its refutation. His argument proceeds as follows: —

Attention is first called to certain modes of the mind's functioning which Davies considers to be essentially different from sense, and then he proceeds to show that the mind cannot be a derivative of sense because of the *sui generis* character of these higher modes of functioning which are expressive of the mind's essential nature. In the first place, the mind has the power of scientific generalization — of gathering —

" From many cases like, one rule of Law."

This work of generalization is not the work of sense. Again, the mind has the power of seeking

6

the causes of things, and this functioning according
to the law of cause and effect is done without the
aid of sense.   Again, the mind has the power of
functioning according to the law of means and
ends, and this power is her own, underived from
sense.   She has the power also of rational imagination, of definition, of argument, of making moral
distinctions — in short, the power of rational intellect and will, and these powers, so far as their
essential nature is concerned, are independent of
sense.   But while thus original and underived from
sense, the mind in these fundamental modes of her
energizing, does not act out of all relation to sense.
Davies approaches close to the Kantian position
here.   The rational soul without sense would be
empty, and sense without the rational soul would
be blind.   Speaking of the soul, in her relation to
sense, he says : —

> " Nor can her selfe discourse or iudge of ought,
>   But what the *Sense* collects and home doth bring
>   And yet the power of her discoursing thought,
>   From these collections, is a diuers thing.

> " For though our eyes can nought but colours see,
>   Yet colours giue them not their powre of sight ;
>   So, though these fruits of *Sense* her obiects bee,
>   Yet she discernes them by her proper light.

" The workman on his stuffe his skill doth show,
  And yet the stuffe giues not the man his skill;
  Kings their affaires do by their seruants know,
  But order them by their owne royall will.

" So, though this cunning mistresse and this queene,
  Doth, as her instrument, the *Senses* vse,
  To know all things that are *felt, heard, or seene,*
  Yet she her selfe doth onely *iudge* and *chuse.*"

After a little further illustration of the difference and relations between sense and soul,
he enters more specifically upon his argument
to prove that the latter is not derived from the
former : —

If the soul be merely " a fine perfection of the
sense," then what is that which accuses sense of
false judgments and of fond appetites, and leads us
to do that which is obnoxious to sense? An analysis of judgment proper and of moral discernment
and choice reveals the fact that their nature is
something other than sense. Again, it is further
evident that there are powers of mind which are
essentially different from sense. If there were not,
then those in whom the senses are sound, should
have sound minds. That is, most of wisdom and
least of folly. However, as a matter of fact, this
is not the case. Wisdom usually comes with age,

and decay of the senses accompanies age. On the other hand, folly usually characterizes those of quickest sense.

Again, if all mental life is, in the final analysis, naught but sense, then animal intelligence would be superior to human intelligence; for animals, as a rule, are possessed of keener sense than man. But animal intelligence is inferior to human intelligence. Animals are wanting in reasoning power — in "that *quicke discoursing power*" by which the erroneous judgments of sense are rectified. This is manifest, for example, in the case of the bee that seeks for honey in the painted flower; and in birds that peck the shadow for the fruit. Again, there is a difference between sense and soul. Sense deals with the forms or externals of things. Soul, on the other hand, penetrates them — grasping their essential natures. But, really, to speak accurately, says the poet, it is incorrect thus to separate sense and soul. Sense is really a power of soul — one aspect of the soul's activity. Through the various senses the soul acquaints herself with the divers forms of objects. While the sense spreads outward, it nevertheless has its root in the soul. Sense in itself would be blind. It could not perceive objects. It is the soul that perceives. Eyes and ears know no more of their objects than do glasses of the faces which they reflect. This is quite evident when we remember that if thought be elsewhere, we often fail to see things even though the eyes be open. And if there were not a unitary power which both sees and hears, our sights and sounds would be double. It is the soul, then, that really perceives.[1] Sense, he repeats, without soul, would be blind; just as the judgments of the soul without the materials of sense would be empty. In view of the foregoing reasons, Davies concludes that the position of Sensationalism is untenable — that the soul is something more than a " fine perfection of the sense " — that it is

[1] Compare these words with those of Cicero, who says: " For not even now is it with our eyes that we view what we see, for the body itself has no senses; but . . . there are certain perforated channels from the seat of the soul to the eyes, ears, and nose; so that frequently, when either prevented by meditation, or the force of some bodily disorder, we neither hear nor see, though our eyes and ears are open and in good condition ; so that we may easily apprehend that it is the soul itself which sees and hears, and not those parts which are, as it were, but windows to the soul, by means of which, however, she can perceive nothing, unless she is on the spot, and exerts herself. How shall we account for the fact that by the same power of thinking we comprehend the most different things — as color, taste, heat, smell, and sound — which the soul could never know by her five messengers, unless everything were referred to her, and she were the sole judge of all." — Op. cit., Bk. I. sec. 20.

a distinct, unitary agent, — sense itself being one
of its modes of functioning: —

> " Then is the *Soule* a nature, which containes
> The powre of *Sense*, within a greater power
> Which doth imploy and vse the *Senses* paines,
> But sits and rules within her priuate bower."

The theory of Sensationalism, which our poet
so earnestly endeavors to refute, is quite conspicuous in the history of speculative thought.
Among the Ancients, it was taught by the Sophists
and the Sceptics. Among the Moderns, Hobbes,
Hume, Condillac, Hartley, James Mill, Comte, John
Stuart Mill, Lewes, Spencer, and others, are its
disciples. There are three aspects or forms of the
theory, the psychological, ontological, and epistemological. Sensationalism from the psychological point of view endeavors to explain all mental
life on the basis of sensations grouped according
to certain mechanical laws, usually called laws of
association. Given the raw materials of sensations,
and combining them according to these laws, all
the higher forms of mental activity, as conception,
judgment, reasoning, willing, etc., can be accounted
for. They are all derivations of sense. Or, beginning analytically with the highest forms of

mental life, by a kind of psychological chemistry we are enabled to analyze them into their ultimate elements — sensations. This psychological aspect of Sensationalism is common to all advocates of the theory.

There is but a short step from the psychological to the ontological aspect of the theory. Viewed from this standpoint, not only all the higher modes of mental life are explainable on the basis of sensations and their mechanical groupings, but the mind itself is thus explained. It has no other being than that of sensations and their ideas, united by the laws of association. There is no unitary subject of conscious states — no unitary, distinct individual agent, manifesting itself in manifold forms of activity, such as perceiving, remembering, thinking, willing, etc. The idea of an agent functioning in certain forms is foreign to these thinkers. Man is merely —

" A willy-nilly current of sensations."

Or, as Hume, the prince of Sensationalists, has put it, " a bundle of perceptions." Sometimes this position is in the interests of an idealistic interpretation of the ultimate nature of reality, as in the case of Hume's philosophy. Again, it favors a materialistic philosophy, as in the case of Spencer

— sensations being conceived as mere modes of nervous motion, or " nervous shocks."

Viewed from an epistemological standpoint, Sensationalism lands us in scepticism or agnosticism. It leads to scepticism by making sense the only source of knowledge. Thus it necessarily implies the relativity of knowledge — that knowledge is relative to each individual, and as each individual differs from every other, there can be no universal factor which real knowledge demands. This is clearly brought out in the philosophy of Protagoras, as embodied in his famous saying, that " Man is the measure of all things " — meaning by man, each individual man, and each individual man in the immediacy and individuality of his character as distinguished from his universal character as revealed in his rationality. In other words, all knowledge being sense knowledge, " and as sensations differ for different individuals, a thing seeming green to one and blue to another, large to one and small to another, it follows that there are as many *truths* as individuals; that the individual is the measure of the true and the false; . . . that there are no universally valid truths or principles, or, at least, that we have no certain criterion (κριτήριον) by which we recognize the absolute truth of a metaphysical or moral proposition. The individual is the measure of the true and the good. . . . It is not possible for us to prove anything but the particular fact of sensation; still more impossible is it to know the causes or ultimate conditions of reality, which escape all sense-perception." [1] Much of our modern agnosticism is based on Sensationalism. It recognizes sensations as the ultimate objects of knowledge. The objects or grounds of these sensations cannot be reached by the human mind. The so-called thought-relations, by which it is supposed we reach the reality beyond sensations, being resolved into relations merely between sensations themselves.

Now, of these three aspects of Sensationalism, Davies deals with the first two — the psychological and the ontological. And he deals with the psychological as leading up to the ontological, with which he is primarily concerned. In his treatment of Sensationalism, he in no respect underestimates its force, but he undoubtedly succeeds in detecting its vulnerable point. In opposition to it, he affirms the reality of the mind as a distinct agent underived from any elementary mind-stuff in the form of sense or sensations.

[1] Weber's " History of Philosophy," trans. by F. Thilly. New York, 1896, pp. 60–61.

The reason for such affirmation, according to him,
is the consciousness of the existence of such an
agent in the exercise of its fundamental powers —
wit and will. The mind's real being consists in
these fundamental modes of psychical functioning,
and these powers cannot be derived from sense,
but are original, underived, native powers of the
soul. That this is so, he affirms, is evident from
the fact that they correct the testimony of sense;
they do what is obnoxious to sense; they lead us
in directions counter to sense; that sense would
be blind without the rational soul; and that, after
all, sense itself is but an aspect or form of the
soul's activity. He views the mind activity-wise,
rather than merely content-wise as does the sen-
sationalist; and insists just as emphatically, although in a much less thorough fashion, as did
Kant in his immortal *Critique of Pure Reason* on
the native activity of mind in its relation to sense.
And he further insists, that this underived mental
activity is the activity of a spiritual or psychical
agent whose existence and essential nature are
revealed in and by this activity itself: —

> " Then her *selfe-being nature* shines in this,
>   That she performes her noblest works alone ;
>   The *worke*, the touch-stone of the *nature* is,
>   And by their operations, things are knowne."

The distinction between sense and the rational soul which Davies insists upon is thoroughly Aristotelian. In his refutation of Sensationalism, and later in his analysis of the powers of the soul, Davies is in accord with three positions of Aristotle: (1) That there is an essential distinction between sense and the rational soul. (2) That the rational soul, unlike sense, is independent of the bodily organism. (3) That the rational soul is " the source of general ideas." On these points Aristotle says: " This consideration shews how improbable it is that reason should be incorporated with the bodily organism: for if so, it would be of some definite character, either hot or cold, or it would have some organ for its operation, just as is the case with sense. But, as matter of fact, reason has nothing of this character. There is truth, too, in the view of those who say the soul is the source of general ideas; only it is soul not as a whole but in its faculty of reason: and the forms or ideas in question exist within the mind, not as endowments which we already possess, but only as capacities to be developed." [1] And he follows with an explanation of the differences between the "faculty of reason" and the " faculty of sense." [2]

[1] Op. cit., Bk. III. ch. iv. sec. 4.   [2] Ibid., secs. 5–8.

CHAPTER V

REALITY OF THE SOUL. — MATERIALISM

THUS far the poet has dealt with Sensationalism. He considers next another theory that
denies the reality of the soul as a distinct, unitary
spiritual agent, — and this is Materialism. Several
forms or aspects of this theory are considered by
Davies, the first of which he indicates in the last
line of the following stanza. Speaking of the soul
he says : —

> " *She is a substance*, and a reall thing,
>   Which hath it selfe an actuall working might;
>   Which neither from the Senses' power doth spring,
>   Nor from the bodie's humors, tempred right."

The theory of Materialism indicated in the
words of the last line of this stanza is undoubtedly
the old theory which identified the soul with the
well-tempered humors of the body, or with the
so-called vital and animal spirits. The blood was
considered the noblest humor, and it was supposed by some that the heart prepared the vital

spirits out of the blood. Then the vital spirits were refined in the cavities of the brain into animal spirits, which were supposed to be the soul or spirit of man. So that this is what Davies means by the words: —

> " How gross are they that drown her in the blood !
> Or in the bodie's humors tempred well."

Against such a conception of the soul Davies urges the following argument: —

Such a conception would mean, that one with the best tempered body would be possessed of the best mind, which would be the same as affirming that the musician with the best instrument, and the best tuned instrument, had the most skill, and that the neat pencil and clear colors made the painter. If we are to thus regard the soul, why does not a beautiful body refine the understanding? Why does not a good complexion rectify the will? Why does not health bring wisdom, and sickness make men brutish? Furthermore, who can find in the faculties of the soul — in memory, or understanding, or will — aught of those original elements, air, fire, earth, or water, from which it is supposed these humors spring? What skillful alchemist can draw the quintessence of

these from the mind? Again, if the lifeless and
senseless elements can produce in us so great a
power as the soul, why do they not give themselves, as well as other things with which they are
mixed, a like excellence? Again, if the soul were
merely a quality of the body, then would she be
sick, maimed, and blind when the body is so.
Instead of this, however, we often find a healthy,
sharp-sighted, perfect soul where these privations
are manifest. If the soul thus partook of the
nature of the body then would her strength decay
with the decay of the strength of the body. But
as a matter of fact, "when the bodie's strongest
sinewes slake," the soul is most active. Again, if
the soul were a mere accident of the body, as
whiteness is an accident of snow, then she might
absent herself from the body without being missed
by the substance thereof. But this is not so. It
is the body that depends on the soul, and not the
soul that depends on the body. It is the soul that
sustains and cherishes the body. It is she that
lends the secret powers of life to it. When these
life-giving powers of the soul are withdrawn, the
body perishes. In short, the physical organism
in itself considered, apart from the soul, is a dead,
inert thing. Hence Davies concludes, that the

soul must not be identified with the well-tempered humors of the body.

" Since then the *Soule works by her selfe alone,*
    Springs not from Sense, nor humors, well agreeing;
    Her nature is peculiar, and her owne :
    She is a *substance,* and a *perfect being.*"

In discussing this theory of the identification of the soul with the well-tempered humors of the body, Davies has probably in mind, as was previously suggested, some form of the doctrine of " spirits " so commonly accepted in the Middle Ages and even after his own time. The doctrine was held in different forms and dates back to Greek and Alexandrine thought. But the form prevalent in medieval times was that of the theory of Galen. Lange says, that " Galen's theory of the psychical and ' animal spiritus ' in connection with the doctrine of the four humors and the temperaments was very early in the Middle Ages fused with the Aristotelian psychology. According to this doctrine, which may be found at full length even in Melancthon's Psychology, the four fundamental humors are prepared in the liver (second organic process after the first has taken place in the stomach) ; out of the noblest humor, the blood, the 'spiritus vitalis' is prepared by a new process in the heart; and this is finally (the fourth and last process) in the cavities of the brain refined into the 'spiritus animalis.'"[1] When our poet, in his refutation of the theory that identifies the soul with the humors, asks the question: —

> " Who can in *memory*, or *wit*, or *will*,
>   Or *ayre*, or *fire*, or *earth*, or *water* finde ?
>   What alchymist can draw, with all his skil,
>   The *quintessence* of these, out of the mind ? "

he has undoubtedly in mind the four elements of Empedocles, to which the chief humors of the body were, by Galen and others before and after him, supposed to correspond.[2]

The crass materialism which identified the mind with these well-tempered humors of the body, was obnoxious to Davies, and he repudiated it, giving his reasons for so doing as stated above. In his refutation of the theory he puts forth a view of the relation of the soul to the body which is exceedingly interesting. According to our poet, it is not

---

[1] " History of Materialism," trans. by E. C. Thomas. Boston, 1877, Vol. I. pp. 237–238.

[2] Cf. J. H. Bass, " Outlines of the History of Medicine," trans. by H. E. Handerson. New York, 1899, pp. 101 sq. and 107 sq.

the soul that is dependent on the body, but rather the body that is dependent on the soul. The very life of the body is derived from the soul. Without the life-giving power of the soul, the body is dead. Death is in fact the withdrawal of the soul from the body. This theory of the relation of soul and body is, however, not original with Davies. It is taught by Nemesius. He says: "All confesse there is a SOUL; and if it be neither a *Body*, nor an *accident*, it is manifest that it is a *substance* without a *body;* and no such thing as cannot stand by it selfe without a subject: For such things may without the destruction of the *subject* be either in the same, or absent; but if the SOUL be separated from the body, that body must of necessity be destroyed." [1]

But this doctrine antedates Nemesius. It is a fundamental point in Aristotle's psychology or rather physiological psychology. He says: "The soul then is the cause and basis of the body as alive; and is so in each of the three senses in which the word cause is used: that is to say it is so both as the efficient cause from which movement springs, as the end or final cause and as the real or essential substance of animate bodies.

[1] Op. cit., p. 182.

7

" That the soul is so as essential substance is evident. In the case of all objects, the cause of their existence constitutes their essential substance. Now it is life which constitutes the existence of all animals, and of these processes of life soul is at once the cause and origin; and further, in the case of something which exists potentially, it is the full realization which is the notion or essential nature.

" It is equally clear that soul is cause in the sense of end or final cause. Like reason, nature acts for the sake of some object; and this object is its end. Now in the animal world the soul is naturally something of this character. All natural bodies are instruments of the soul: and just as it is with the bodies of animals so also is it with those of plants, all being there simply for the sake of soul. But in saying that the soul is the end or final cause, we must remember that the word ' end ' is used in two senses, and must understand it as meaning that at which a thing aims quite as much as that for which it exists.

" Lastly, the soul is also cause as being the original source of local movement, a faculty however which all creatures do not have. The soul also exhibits phenomena of alteration and augmen-

tation: for sensation is held to be a form of alteration and nothing possesses this faculty of sense
unless it participate in soul. So also is it with
augmentation and decay: nothing decays or grows
in a natural manner except it receive nutrition:
and nothing is nurtured except it partake of life." [1]

[1] Op. cit., Bk. II. ch. iv. secs. 3–6.

CHAPTER VI

NATURE OF THE SOUL. — MATERIALISM

HAVING thus endeavored to vindicate the claims of the soul to a being of her own, he proceeds to explain the nature of the soul. Here again he crosses swords with the Materialist. He affirms the soul to be a spirit — not, however, like the air or wind, nor like the so-called "vital spirits," nor like the spirits spoken of by the alchemists. She surpasses "all *natures* vnder heauen." She is like the spirits or heavenly intelligences who behold the face of God. Yea, she is like God herself, originally bearing his image, but having degenerated to such an extent as to scarcely now constitute his shadow. She is superior to all "formes" knit to bodies. But although joined to the body, she is "*bodilesse* and free," and though confined, she is almost infinite. She cannot be a body, for if so, how could she be contained in the body which is not so great as she — how could she contain "the world's great shape"

— how could she reflect or mirror the world? Bodies are subject to space relations — not so with the soul. Instead of being confined to place, she herself contains all places. It is impossible for bodies to admit two forms at once without one defacing the other; but the soul can admit ten thousand forms, none intruding upon its neighbor's place. All bodies are filled with other bodies. The soul's "wide imbracements" cannot be filled, for its capacity increases by acquisition. Things take the proportions of things receiving them : —

"So little glasses little faces make,
And narrow webs on narrow frames be weau'd."

But not so with the soul. If she were a body, how vast she would have to be to contain, as she does, all sorts of corporeal objects, as, "men, beasts, trees, towns, seas, and lands" : —

"And yet each thing a proper place doth find,
And each thing in the true proportion stands."

This were impossible to the mind were it not for the fact that by some strange sublimation she converts bodies into spirits. She abstracts the forms from material bodies — she draws a sort of "*quintessence* from things," which she transforms into her own nature. This is manifest in her

abstraction of universals from particular objects —
which universals are bodiless and immaterial in
their character and find a lodgment only in minds.
Again, were the mind a body it would be impossible for her to know several bodies, just as it is
impossible for a mirror not free from all forms to
reflect several faces. Our eyes could not discern
all colors if they were not themselves void of
colors. Again, the quick movements of the mind
show her to be a spirit. She travels immense
distances in a moment of time. It is impossible
for a body to do so. The conclusion is, that
the soul is not a corporeal or bodily thing, but
rather an incorporeal, immaterial thing — a spiritual
agent : —

> " As then the *Soule* a substance hath alone,
>   Besides the Body in which she is confin'd;
>   So hath she not a *body* of her owne,
>   But is a *spirit*, and *immateriall minde*."

In the preceding consideration of Materialism
Davies gives no exposition of the doctrine. He
merely refutes the notion of regarding the soul
as a bodily thing. He may have in mind either
the views of Democritus, the Stoics, the Epicureans, or Lucretius; or, indeed, the views of

all of these philosophers; for all of them affirm
the soul to be corporeal in its nature. Nemesius,
in refuting this theory, refers to all of the above
mentioned thinkers, except Lucretius.[1] Davies
in dealing with Materialism makes use of two
arguments used by Nemesius, in discussing the
relation of soul and body, namely, (1) That body
is confined to place, whereas the soul is not.
(2) That body has dimensions, but the soul has
none. Nemesius says: " For, as the *Sun*, so soon
as it appeareth, changes the *ayre* into *light;* so
making it lightsome, and so diffusing it selfe with
the *ayre*, that it is united with the same, and yet
not confounded therewith: Even so, the *soul* being united with the *Body*, remaines without confusion therewith; differing in this onely, that the
Sunne being a *Body*, and circumscribed within
the compasse of *Place*, is not himselfe in every
place where his *light* is, but (as *fire* in the *wood*,
or as the *flame* in a *candle*) is confined to a certaine *place*.

" It is not so with the *soul*. For, being void
of all *Body*, and not contained within the limits
of any place, it passeth *all* and *whole*, through
its own whole *light*, and through the whole *Body*,

[1] Op. cit., pp. 77–113.

wherein it is; neither is any part of it illuminated thereby, wherein it is not fully and wholly present. Neither is it in the *body* as in some bottle or other vessell, nor compassed in by the same; but the *Body* is rather in the *soule*, and is thereby held in and fastned together.

"For, *intelligible things* (such as the *soul* is) are not hindred by *bodily things;* but, enter, and pierce, and pass through every *corporeall* thing, and cannot possibly bee contained within the circumference of a *bodily-place*. Things *intellectuall*, have their being in places also *intelligible;* yea they are either in *themselves*, or else in such *intellectuall things*, as are above themselves.

"The *soul* is otherwhile in it *selfe;* as, when it *reasoneth* or considereth of things; and otherwhile in the *understanding;* as, when it conceiveth any thing: And when it is said to bee in the *body*, it is not said to be there, as in *place ;* but, to be as it were in a certaine *relation* to the *body;* and to bee present with it in such a sense, as, God is said to be in *us*." [1]

Thus far Nemesius shows that body is confined to place; but not so with the soul. And he further points out that body has dimensions, but

[1] Op. cit., pp. 197–200.

the soul has not: "For," he continues, "wee say
that the *soul* is bound (as it were) by a certaine
disposition and inclination, as the *lover* is to his
beloved: not bound in place, or as *bodies* are
bound; but by the habituall bands of *affection*.
And indeed, seeing it hath neither *magnitude*,
nor *massinesse*, nor *parts*, how can it be enclosed
by a speciall *place ?* Or within what *place* can
that bee contained, which hath no *parts ?* Where
place is, there must needs bee a *massinesse;* because *place* is the *Bound* which compasseth
another thing; and hath its being in respect of
that which it encloseth." [1]

Davies argues similarly, but more briefly : —

> " All *bodies* are confin'd within some place,
> But *she* all place within her selfe confines ;
> All *bodies* haue their measure, and their space,
> But who can draw the *Soule's* dimensiue lines? "

It would seem, especially in view of what will
appear later, that here again Davies had recourse
to Nemesius.

The last argument against regarding the soul
as body, which Davies makes use of, based on
the swiftness of the soul's movements, may be
found also in Calvin. The theologian, in endeav-

[1] Op. cit., pp. 200-201.

oring to show that the soul cannot be identified
with body, says: "But the swiftness with which
the human mind glances from heaven to earth,
scans the secrets of nature, and, after it has embraced all ages, with intellect and memory digests
each in its proper order, and reads the future in
the past, clearly demonstrates that there lurks in
man a something separated from the body."[1]

Davies says: —

"If lastly, this quicke power a body were,
    Were it as swift as is the *winde* or *fire ;*
    (Whose atomies doe th' one down side-waies beare,
    And make the other in *pyramids* aspire :)

"Her nimble body yet in time must moue,
    And not in instants through all places slide ;
    But she is nigh, and farre, beneath, aboue,
    In point of time, which thought cannot deuide:

"She is sent as soone to *China* as to *Spaine*,
    And thence returnes, as soone as shee is sent;
    She measures with one time, and with one paine,
    An ell of silke, and heauen's wide spreading tent."

Davies's refutation of Materialism is, of course,
crude.   But we must remember that he was dealing with a crude Materialism.   It was not such
a doctrine as we meet with in nineteenth and
twentieth century scientific Materialism.   It was

[1] Op. cit., Bk. I. ch. xv. sec. 2.

not a theory formed in the light of the doctrines of the conservation of energy, and biological evolution, or in the light of modern brain physiology. Davies took Materialism as he found it, and met its disciples on their own ground, — how successfully the reader may judge for himself. But in taking his stand on the side of a spiritualistic philosophy — in affirming the reality of mind as distinguished from matter, he has identified himself with the main current of speculative thought. In carefully reviewing the history of philosophy one cannot fail to be impressed with the poverty of Materialism. As compared with a spiritualistic philosophy — either in the form of Dualism or Idealism — it plays an inferior part in the history of speculative thought. It is true it had a flourishing career in Greek and Græco-Roman thought. But as one compares pre-Socratic materialistic philosophy with the Socratic, Platonic, and Aristotelian philosophy, in which the spiritual nature of mind is recognized, he will be impressed with the poverty of the former and the richness of the latter. Likewise, if he makes a comparison between the Stoic and Epicurean Materialism and the philosophy of Socrates, Plato, and Aristotle a similar impression prevails. Ancient Materialism is not rich in great names or great systems. Again, for fifteen centuries of the Christian era Materialism had scarcely a representative of note.[1] Indeed, from Epicurus and Lucretius to Descartes — the founder of modern philosophy — it hardly receives mention by historians of philosophy. Whereas, much of early Christian philosophy, and Scholastic philosophy also, were, of course, spiritualistic in character. The case is essentially the same in Modern as in Ancient Philosophy. From Descartes through Spinoza, Malebranche, Geulincx, Leibnitz, and Wolff, to Kant, on the Continent; and from Locke, through Berkeley, and Hume (Idealistic Sensationalism), to Reid, in Great Britain, philosophy has either been dualistic or idealistic — affirming in either case the reality of mind. During this period, Materialism was represented by Gassendi, Hobbes, Toland, Priestley, the Encyclopædists (?), La Mettrie, and d'Holbach. To the student of the history of philosophy the two movements of thought hardly admit of comparison so far as their significance is concerned. The former is the great stream

---

[1] There was more or less Materialism in early Christian speculative thought. This was doubtless due to a considerable extent to the influence of the Stoics.

of modern speculative thought flowing in this period; the latter is a small current flowing alongside or through it. And, if anything, the contrast is more marked in the history of philosophical thought from Kant to the present day. The dominant character of philosophy since Kant has been idealistic. The great systems of Fichte, Schelling, Hegel, Schopenhauer, Von Hartmann, and Lotze, testify to this fact. They pre-eminently constitute the main current of Modern Philosophy. Dualism also during this period, as manifest in the development of Scottish philosophy from Reid to Hamilton, constitutes no insignificant current. True, this period witnessed the birth of a more "scientific" Materialism than that of preceding thought. The rapid development of the natural sciences, the wide acceptance of the theories of evolution, and of the correlation of forces, the mechanical explanation of phenomena, and the progress in nerve and brain physiology — all of these things gave rise to a materialistic view of the world and the soul. The more speculative representatives of this movement in Germany were Moleschott, Vogt, Büchner, Haeckel, and others. In France it has had comparatively few representatives of note. Probably Cabanis may be called its most distinguished exponent there. And it may be questioned whether he really teaches a philosophical Materialism. In Great Britain Materialism is taught more by implication than as a scientific or philosophical dogma. It is certainly an implication of the teachings of Spencer and Huxley, and possibly of Tyndall. Professor Flint accurately states the case as follows: " In England, Mr. Herbert Spencer, Professors Huxley and Tyndall, and a few other writers of distinguished philosophical or scientific talents, have done far more to diffuse materialism than any of those who are willing to avow themselves materialists. Never was materialism more fortunate than when it secured to itself the sympathy and support of minds so vigorous and so richly gifted." [1]

This, briefly, and in a general way, has been the history of Materialism as compared with Dualism and Idealism. Its comparative poverty of history is due to the inherent poverty of its cause. The utter inability thus far of even a so-called " scientific " Materialism to explain conscious life on the basis of the molecular activity of the brain; the

[1] "Anti-Theistic Theories." Edinburgh and London, 1877, Appendix, Note xv.

utter unlikeness of neural and psychic activity
when subjected to the closest and most thorough
examination, make, in the writer's judgment, the
words of Du Bois-Reymond eminently true: " I
will now prove conclusively, as I believe, that not
only is consciousness unexplained by material conditions in the present state of our science (which all
will admit), but that, in the very nature of things, it
never can be explained by these conditions. The
most exalted mental activity is no more incomprehensible in its material conditions than is the first
grade of consciousness—namely, sensation. With
the first awakening of pleasure and pain experienced upon earth by some creature of the simplest
structure appeared an impassable gulf, and the
world became doubly incomprehensible." [1]

We have seen, then, that Davies in affirming the
essential reality of the psychic in opposition to
Materialism is in the current of the world's profoundest thought. But in his efforts to vindicate
the essential selfhood or being of the soul, he failed
to deal with a more formidable opposition than
Materialism, namely, Pantheistic Idealism; or,
better, Idealistic Pantheism. Such Pantheism is a

---

[1] "Ueber die Grenzen des Naturerkennens," pp. 20, 21.
Quoted from Flint, op. cit., Appendix, Note xviii.

thorough-going Monism — affirming mind to be
the only reality, but cancelling the reality of the
finite mind — it being merely a mode of the Absolute, or the Absolute coming to consciousness.
At best, then, the finite mind has merely a phe-
nomenal existence. It has no being-for-self — no
real selfhood. Of such a theory Davies hardly
seems conscious. At least he does not consider
it. And yet, in a philosophy of mind, it is not
sufficient to prove the reality of the spiritual or
psychic as against the claims of Materialism; but
also, if possible, to vindicate the right of the
human soul to a being of its own, in opposition
to the claims of Idealistic Pantheism. The latter
undertaking is a much more difficult task than the
former.

Davies's conception of the essential reality and
individuality of the soul is more in harmony with
Christian theology than with Greek Philosophy.
In this respect he was probably influenced more
by Nemesius and Calvin and his general Christian
teaching than by Greek thought. For in Greek
Philosophy the distinction between the human soul
and the Divine Intelligence, and the World-Soul,
is nowhere as sharply drawn as it is in Davies's
philosophy, especially as involved in his doctrine

of creation, which he presents later. Nor is the
distinction between soul and body as sharply defined by Aristotle, to whom our poet was so much
indebted, as in Davies's thought. Such views as
he expresses on this subject represent in the main
the prevailing thought of Christian Theology from
Augustine to the present day (with some notable
exceptions). Since Augustine, Christian Theology in its ontology has not, as a rule, been monistic. It has usually taught the existence of three
distinct realities, — God, the created material world
(including the animal and human organism), and
the created human soul. This is undoubtedly the
view that underlies Davies's philosophy.

If we turn to Modern Philosophy, we find that,
in the pre-Kantian period, the essential being or
individuality of the soul is affirmed by Descartes,[1]
Malebranche,[2] Leibnitz,[3] Wolff,[4] Locke,[5] Berkeley,[6]
Reid,[7] and other philosophers of less distinction.
Kant himself, in the *Critique of Pure Reason* (in

[1] "Second Meditation."

[2] "De la Recherche de la Verite," Liv. III. ii. 1–3.

[3] "Monadology." See also "Letter to Wagner on the Active
Force of Body, on the Soul," etc.

[4] "Latin Works: Psychologia rationalis."

[5] "Essay on Human Understanding," Bk. II., ch. xxvii.

[6] "Principles of Human Knowledge."

[7] "Essays on the Intellectual Powers of Man," Essay I. ch. iv.

the Transcendental Dialectic especially), regards the soul as a noumenon — a transcendental reality — a reality unknown to the pure reason. But in the *Critique of Practical Reason* he makes the soul and its immortality a reality known through the practical reason or moral consciousness. From Kant to Von Hartmann German philosophy is mainly Idealistic Pantheism. In the philosophy of Fichte, and also of Hegel, Schopenhauer, and Von Hartmann, the human soul is in some way or other identified with the Absolute.[1] It is not regarded as having a real, distinct being of its own. Since Kant, Lotze is probably the most distinguished German philosopher who has maintained the self-being of the finite soul.[2]

The above briefly indicates the attitude of the more important philosophical and theological thought towards the position which Davies so positively affirmed; namely, the spiritual self-being of the human soul.

[1] Cf. Windelband, " A History of Philosophy," trans. by J. H. Tufts, 2d ed., Chicago, 1900, Pt. VI. ch. ii., for a brief account of the development of German Idealism.

[2] See especially his " Mikrokosmus," II Buch, c. 1, 2.

CHAPTER VII

ORIGIN OF THE SOUL IN CONNECTION WITH THE BODY

FROM the discussion of the reality and nature of the soul, the poet turns to the consideration of that difficult and much mooted question (especially in theological circles) of the mode of the soul's origin. How does the soul come into being? Assuming, as Davies does, that it has its ultimate origin in God, the real question with him is, the origin of the soul in its connection with the body. He considers three theories of the origin of the soul — Pre-existence, Creationism, and Traducianism. The Church Father, Origen, in his commentary on Canticles, has given a very clear statement of the nature of these theories. He says: " The question is, first, whether the human spirit is created, or has existed from the beginning (pre-existence); next, if created, whether it was created once for all, and connected in such a way with the body as to be propagated, along with it, by natural generation (traducianism), or whether it is created successively, and, in each individual case, added from without, in order to vivify the body forming in the womb (creationism)." [1]

Of these three theories, Davies accepts Creationism, with a slight modification of the form presented by Origen. In taking this position, he at first merely states the theory and his acceptance of it, without an argument to substantiate his views. The reasons for its acceptance are presented later. He states his own position as follows : —

> " *Since body and soule* haue such diuersities,
>   Well might we muse, how first their match began,
>   But that we learne, that He that spread the skies,
>   And fixt the Earth, first form'd the *soule* in man.

> " This true *Prometheus* first made Man of earth,
>   And shed in him a beame of heauenly fire ;
>   Now in their mother's wombs before their birth,
>   Doth in all sonnes of men their *soules* inspire.

> " And as *Minerua* is in fables said,
>   From *Ioue*, without a mother to proceed ;
>   So our true *Ioue*, without a mother's ay'd,
>   Doth daily millions of *Mineruas* breed."

In other words, every individual soul is an absolute, immediate creation on the part of God; and

[1] Schaff-Herzog Religious Encyclopædia, etc. **New York,** 1882, Vol. I. pp. 569–570.

is breathed into the body with which it is to be associated while yet in the mother's womb. Violent as this hypothesis is, it seems much more acceptable to him than either of the opposing theories.

With this statement of his position, he first considers the doctrine of Pre-existence. He argues, that God did not create all souls at once, either " from eternitie before," or " from the time when *Time's* first point begun," which he keeps in some other sphere, or housed in some secret cloister, until the day of their marriage with the body. Neither is that form of the theory which involves the transmigration of souls, or metempsychosis, true. God did not first create a number of souls, —

" Infusing part in *beasts*, and part in *men*,"

and so ordain that at the death of the body the soul should be married to another body, —

" And so by often changing and supplying,
  Men's *soules* to beasts, and beasts to men did passe."

This theory must be repudiated. Were it true, thousands of bodies " must be abortiue, and forlorne," before they receive souls through the death of other bodies, because the number of bodies born exceeds by far the number of bodies that die.

Over against this theory of Pre-existence and
metempsychosis, Davies sets his own theory of
Creationism.   Just as Nature, God's handmaid,
creates bodies in distinct time, and in due order, —

> " So God giues *soules* the like successiue date,
>   Which Himselfe makes, in bodies formèd new."

He strongly emphasizes the supposed fact that
God himself creates the soul, and does so directly
— not through secondary causes.   He does not
delegate this power either to angels or to Nature.
Especially does he call attention to the fact that
Nature's services are not utilized in bringing the
soul into being.   For, although she can derive
bodies from bodies, she could never derive souls
from souls.   This would be an impossibility.

After thus again affirming the Creationist's view,
he takes into consideration the objection urged
against this theory by Traducianism.   There were
those — revered Church Fathers — " great lights
of old " — whose eyes were dimmed with religious
fear, who opposed the doctrine of Creationism,
substituting for it the doctrine of Traducianism.
The religious fear which constituted the ground of
their objection, arose from the supposed bearing
of this view on the doctrine of original sin.   The
poet interprets this objection as follows : —

We are taught by Rule of Faith that every soul united to a human body is born in sin — bringing the " sinne of kind " from the mother's womb.   To affirm that God creates the soul directly, and not through secondary causes, is to make him author of the soul's sin, for sin began in the soul of man. If the soul of man is by nature corrupt, as the dogma of original sin affirms, and if we hold that it is an immediate creation of God, then we affirm either that God first creates it corrupt, which seems sacrilegious, or that the body corrupts it. But the body, of itself, has no such power.   It was the soul, and not the body, of Adam that sinned, and thus brought corruption to itself.   And the soul born to-day suffers the consequences.   It participated in Adam's sin.   It comes into being corrupt — it is corrupt before it sins in act or thought.   This being so, God can only be relieved of the responsibility for man's original sin — for man's natural corruption, on the supposition or ground that every human soul is a derivation from the parent soul through propagation.   And this is what Traducianism affirms.   It affirms, also, that Creationism, on the other hand, logically implies responsibility on the part of God for original sin; that is, for the supposed fact that every man is born in sin.

This is the objection of Traducianism. Davies now argues for Creationism, giving reasons for belief in this doctrine, and endeavoring to meet the objection of Traducianism with reference to the bearing of the doctrine of original sin on it.

No one, he says, is so gross as to contend, that the soul is derived from the body. But many subtle minds have contended that souls spring from other souls. This view, however, is erroneous. There are reasons which evidence this. These reasons the poet sets forth as follows: —

All created things are either created from nothing, or from ready-made stuff. No creature ever formed aught from nothing. Such power belongs alone to God. If then a soul beget a soul, it must beget it from stuff or matter. But the soul contains no such matter. If the soul be not created from matter, it must be created from nothing. But, as has been stated, God alone possesses such power. Hence, one finite soul cannot create another.

Again, if souls possess the power of begetting souls, then they must do so either by an exercise of their own power or by an exercise of the power of the body. If by their own power, what should hinder them creating souls every hour? If by the body's power, why can reason and will unite with the body only in this one specific act, since they "abstract" themselves from the body in the performance of other offices or functionings?

Again, such a view makes against the immortality of the soul, for it predicates change and motion of the soul, and change and motion bear the marks of corruption, that is, of destructibility.

Again, if souls beget other souls, then the seed they sow should be incorruptible, that is, indestructible.[1] What then becomes of seed sown in acts of generation from which there is no issue?

Furthermore, only mortal things desire to beget other beings so as to immortalize their kind or perpetuate their species. Souls being immortal, would, therefore, even though possessed of the power of begetting other souls, not exercise it, because as immortal they would not be impelled by a desire to immortalize their kind. Hence, angels, who are immortal, do not marry. The conclusion is, that *God*, and not man, is the creator of spirits.

But what of the objection of the Traducianist? Davies considers the objection at length, and en-

---

[1] Davies here assumes the natural immortality of the soul.

deavors to reconcile Creationism with the dogma
of original sin. God, he argues, created the soul
pure and joined it to the body. However, its
union with the body does not corrupt it. Still
it is corrupt — even in the mother's womb. It
is corrupt even before it can judge or choose.
But God is not the author of this corruption.
From all eternity He decreed all things. He
decreed that every man should be and live his
life. He decreed all human souls to be, and to be
incarnate. This eternal plan or decree was not
to be set aside by the prospect or certainty of
sin. If we knew God's purpose in creation this
discordant element of man's sin might be seen to
make for rather than against harmony. If we
could see how death is the result of sin, but also
"how from *death*, a better *life* doth rise"; and
how this teaches the justice and mercy of God,
we should praise his decree "as right and wise."
But the trouble is, that we must see part by part,
instead of having an intuition of the whole. We
must see things successively instead of simul-
taneously. God, however, sees things differently.
His sight is not of things in part, or in succession,
or in degrees. With Him all things and all events
are an immediate vision. It is the whole that

stands immediately before His gaze. He sees
"*all* men as *one* Man." He sees them as a tree
of which Adam is the root and his heirs the
branches. If the root be corrupted, the branches
will partake of the corruption. Or, He sees all
men as a river, of which Adam is the well or
fountain-head, and his posterity the streams. Pol-
lute the fountain-head, and the streams partake
of the pollution. This is really the kind of head-
ship there is in Adam. This is the manner in
which his sin extends to us. It is not personal
sin. It is "sinne of kind," for we are partakers
of his nature. It is hereditary sin. And it is
because our natures are "parts" of his nature,
that the guilt and punishment of his sin pass to
us "by course of Nature, and of Law." By
course not only of Nature, but also of Law, for
Law makes no distinction between whole and
part: —

> " So was the first transgression generall,
>   And all did plucke the fruit and all did tast."

We have a reflection of this Divine Law in human
law, where thousands of men are regarded as one
man — all bound together in " one Corporation."
These thousands and their successors constitute
but *one*, and, as the former gain or lose, they not

only harm or profit themselves, but also the latter. In other words, human law visits the punishment and rewards of parents upon their children and their children's children — treating all as one. Yet we call not this unjust on the part of man. Shall we then accuse God because of His decree whereby the descendants of Adam partake of the guilt and penalty of his sin?

And now what really constitutes this original sin or "sinne of kind"? It is the deprivation of the soul of the native virtues and powers which God gave to Adam and his race. These constituted God's grace to man. The withdrawal of this grace results in a "*declining pronenesse unto nought.*" Furthermore, being thus deprived of her native virtues, vices spring up to take their places.

But by what means are Adam's descendants thus deprived of these native virtues and made subject to these vices, if God himself immediately creates each soul? The poet answers, that God creates each soul fair and good, but when it unites with the body, which union constitutes the man, who is Adam's heir, then God withdraws his grace from it. It thus loses its "rich dowry" of native virtues, and vices grow up in their stead. And this is not unjust on the part of God.

For, if a man receive " on light conditions " a large estate for himself and heirs, who bemoans the heirs, or blames the giver, if the man wilfully forfeits it?

Nor is this inheritance of sin a strange thing in the light of God's redemptive action in Christ, whose justice and grace are imparted to those who are unjust and without grace.

And, lastly, it were better for the soul to be born a slave to sin, rather than not exist at all. Since, by faith she may be set free, and " mount the higher for her fall."

Still it may be asked, if God foresaw men's fall, why did he not prevent it? The answer is, that this were to cancel man's personality. In other words, it were to declare that " *Man no man shall bee.*" For free will or self-determination is of the very essence of personality : —

> " For what is Man without a moouing mind,
> Which hath a iudging *wit*, and chusing *will* ? "

God made man to know and love his Maker. But a forced, involuntary love could never be grateful or thankworthy. Furthermore, if we were possessed of unchangeable will and unerring wit, we should be guilty of self-esteem. Again, if man were unchangeable, he must either be God, " or

like a root or tree," for even the angels are more
unstable and had a greater fall than man. Let
us be thankful then that we are men, and rest
content, knowing that curiosity was man's fall,
and let us admire the unknowable counsels of
God. And further —

> " let vs know that God the Maker is
> Of all the *Soules*, in all the men that be;
> Yet their corruption is no fault of His,
> But the first man's that broke God's first decree."

Thus the poet disposes of the objection of
Traducianism to Creationism growing out of the
dogma of original sin. Davies finds no difficulty
in his own mind of freeing God from responsibility for man's supposed birth in sin. On this
much mooted question of theology, then, concerning the mode of the soul's origin in its relation to the body, Davies contends that every soul
is an immediate creation on the part of God, on
occasion of the conception of a body, and is united
to the body in its pre-natal state.

The question of the origin of the soul in its
relation to the body has been largely, although not
exclusively, associated with the problem of sin in
the history of speculative thought. The theory of

Pre-existence, as well as the theories of Creationism and Traducianism, has been brought forward
as a probable explanation of this difficult question.
The doctrine of Pre-existence figures more or less
conspicuously in Greek philosophy. It can be
traced to Pythagoras and his school. Herodotus
says that the Greeks borrowed it from the Egyp-
tians.[1] But this statement is open to question, as
the doctrine was an Orphic tradition. With the
Pythagoreans the soul, prior to its incarnation,
existed in a higher realm. The transmigration
of souls was associated with evil doing. Souls
descended into bodies of animals as a punishment
for sin.[2] Zeller, one of the ablest and most reli-
able of historians of Greek philosophy, attributes
the doctrine also to Heracleitus, one of the early
Greek philosophers.[3] The doctrine is also taught
by Empedocles in his famous philosophical poem
entitled *On Nature.* In the teaching of this poet-
philosopher the doctrine is also associated with
sin. We next find the doctrine taught by Plato.
Although it is taught in a number of his works, it
is in the *Phædo* that we find an especially interest-

[1] Bk. II. 123.

[2] " Diogenes Laërtius," Bk. VIII. 19.

[3] " Pre-Socratic Philosophy," trans. by S. F. Alleyne. London, 1881, Vol. II. p. 87.

ing development of it.[1]   Plato founds the doctrine
on the fact of recollection, or reminiscence.   He
represents Cebes in his conversation with Socrates
as saying: "Your favorite doctrine, Socrates, that
knowledge is simply recollection, if true, also necessarily implies a previous time in which we learned
that which we now recollect.   But this would be
impossible unless our soul was in some place
before existing in the human form."[2]   We are
taught in this doctrine of recollection that our
sense-perceptions are copies of Ideas which the
soul perceived in a pre-existent state.   But Plato's
doctrine also involves a migration of souls as a
penalty for sin — a migration through human and
animal bodies.[3]   Later, Pre-existence is taught by
the Neo-Pythagoreans, whose anthropology is essentially that of Plato.[4]   Still later it is found in
the works of Philo Judæus, who was greatly influenced by Plato.   In Philo Pre-existence is associated with the fact of sin.   His teaching involves
transmigration   as   a   punishment   and   means   of

---

[1] Cf. "Phædo," 73.

[2] "The Dialogues of Plato, Phædo," trans. by B. Jowett.
New York, 1885, Vol. I. p. 399.

[3] "Phædo," 81, 82 sq.

[4] Zeller, "Outlines of the History of Greek Philosophy,"
trans. by Alleyne and Abbott.   New York, 1886, p. 309.

purification.[1]   Again, there is quite an elaborate development of the doctrine in Plotinus, who also reveals the influence of Plato.   According to him the soul in the pre-existent state was powerfully impelled from within itself to the body.   Its incarnation represents a moral Fall.[2]   Porphyry taught migration of souls from human bodies to other human bodies.[3]

When we turn to Christian thought we find the doctrine taught by the Church Father, Origen. He was also under the influence of Greek thought. The soul, according to him, sinned in a pre-existent state, and its incarnation is the penalty for its sin.[4] It may be found also in the writings of Cyril of Alexandria,[5] Nemesius,[6] and Prudentius.[7]

In Jewish literature there are, in the *Talmud*, suggestions of a doctrine of pre-existence in the form of souls existing archetypally in the Divine

---

[1] "The Works of Philo Judæus," trans. by C. D. Yonge, London, 1854; cf. especially "A Treatise on the Giants," Vol. I. secs. 2 and 3, also, "A Treatise on the Doctrine that Dreams are Sent from God," Vol. II. Bk. I. sec. 22.

[2] "Ennead," IV. 6.

[3] Augustine, "De Civitate Dei," X. 30.

[4] "De Principiis," I. c. vii. 4, 5.

[5] "Commentarium in Evangelium Joannis," IV.

[6] "De Natura Hominis," c. ii.

[7] "Liber Cathemerinon," X. v.

mind; and, in the Middle Ages, we find it taught as a positive doctrine in the *Kabbala*[1] and certain Rabbinical writings.   Indeed, here the doctrine assumes essentially the form of the doctrine which Davies refutes; namely, a storehouse of pre-exist-ent souls destined to occupy human bodies.

This briefly is the history of the doctrine of Pre-existence prior to the time of our poet.   It is interesting to note that it appears again later in English literature.   Henry More revives it in his philosophical poem on the *Immortality of the Soul* (II. 12).   It is not uncommon in nineteenth cen-tury English poetry, although here it is not asso-ciated with a doctrine of sin.   It is to be found in one of its Platonic aspects in Wordsworth's *Inti-mations of Immortality from Recollections of Early Childhood*.   It is brought forward by Tennyson in *The Two Voices* (even in its transmigration aspect), *De Profundis*, *Idylls of the King*, and *The Ancient Sage*.   Browning affirms it in his *Cristina*, and Mrs. Browning suggests it in *Aurora Leigh*. We even find it taught in recent German theol-ogy.   Julius Müller in his *Lehre von der Sünde*,[2] teaches a moral Fall of man in a timeless state. As we have seen, Davies could not accept the

---

[1] "Zohar," I. 19.   [2] IV. c. iv. §§ 1–3.

doctrine. To him it was an unsatisfactory theory of the origin of the soul in its connection with the body. He disposes of it with little argumentation, and puts in its stead the doctrine of a successive creation of souls to parallel a successive formation of bodies — each soul uniting with the body as it is formed in the mother's womb: —

> " But as *God's handmaid*, *Nature*, doth create
>   Bodies in time distinct, and order due ;
>   So God giues *soules* the like successiue date,
>   Which *Himselfe* makes, in bodies formèd new."

Creationism and Traducianism have played a much more important part in the history of speculative thought than has the doctrine of Pre-existence. They have been associated with the dogma of original sin in Christian theology. Creationism found wide acceptance in early Christian speculative thought. Clement of Alexandria taught the doctrine.[1] It was held also by Lactantius.[2] It was advocated by Theodoret,[3] also by Hilary.[4] On the other hand, Tertullian taught Traducianism — defending it on both philosophical

---

[1] " Stromata," VI. 16.
[2] " Institutiones Divinæ," III. 18.
[3] " Græcarum Affectionum Curatio," V.
[4] " Tractatus super Psalmos," XLI. 3.

and scriptural grounds.[1] It was maintained also
by Gregory of Nyssa;[2] also by Athanasius.[3]
Augustine is not explicit in his teaching concerning the question of the mode of the soul's origin
in connection with the body. He did not commit
himself positively to either doctrine. However,
his doctrine of sin seems to imply Traducianism.[4]

Among the Schoolmen the verdict was almost
unanimous in favor of Creationism. Among the
more prominent of these famous thinkers who
favored the doctrine were: Anselm,[5] Hugo of St.
Victor,[6] Bonaventura,[7] and Thomas Aquinas.[8]

In the sixteenth century Creationism was still
the favorite doctrine in Catholic circles. This is
also the case in Protestant Theology despite the
fact that Luther leaned toward Traducianism.

Creationism was early affirmed by the *Formula
Concordiæ*[9] and the doctrine is usually attributed

[1] "De Anima," XXV.

[2] "De Hominis Opificio," XXIX.

[3] "Oratio contra Arianos," II. 48.

[4] "De Civitate Dei," XI.–XIII.; also "De Gratia Christi
et de Peccato Originali."

[5] "De Conceptu Virginali," VII.

[6] "De Sacramentis Christianæ Fidei," I. vii.

[7] "Breviloq." III. 6.

[8] "Summa Theologiæ," I. 118.

[9] Arts. I., II.

to Calvin, although he is not very pronounced in his views.[1] The Reformed theologians, however, generally taught the doctrine. In the seventeenth century Traducianism was quite universally accepted among Lutheran theologians. Prominent among these were Gerhard,[2] of the University of Jena, Caloveus,[3] of Wittenberg, and Hollaz,[4] of Jacobshagen. On the other hand the Calvinists favored Creationism. Since the seventeenth century there has been a great difference of opinion in the Protestant world, often, indeed, in the same denomination.[5] Of late years a theory has been advanced by Martensen and Dorner, which is of the nature of a compromise. The former holds that there is a truth in both Creationism and Traducianism.[6] And Dorner even combines the doctrine of Pre-existence with Creationism and Traducianism. He says: "Each one of these theories represents *one* aspect of the *whole* truth, — Traducianism generic consciousness, Pre-exist-

1 "Institutes of the Christian Religion," Vol. I. Bk. II. ch. i.

2 "Loci Theologiæ," IX. 8, 116–117.

8 "Systema Locorum Theolog.," etc., III. Art. V. 2.

4 "Examen Theologicum," etc., I. 5.

5 Compare, for example, such recent writers as Hodge, "Systematic Theology," II. iii. 3, and Shedd, "Dogmatic Theology," II. i.

6 "Dogmatics," trans., pp. 162–163.

entianism self-consciousness or the interest of the
personality as a separate eternal divine thought,
. . . Creationism God-consciousness.   Nothing
but the union of these three elements is sufficient.
But the union must not be so conceived as if there
were a mechanical division of the process between
God, the genus, and the element of personality." [1]

This briefly has been the course of thought on
this question of the origin of the soul in its relation to the body.   Davies in adopting the theory
of Creationism was undoubtedly influenced by sixteenth century theology.   Especially is Calvin's
influence manifest in his thinking on this subject,
and more particularly so in his somewhat elaborate
consideration of the objection of Traducianism to
Creationism based on the dogma of original sin.
A comparison of the views of the theologian and
poet on this point will make this evident: —

In the first place, they agree in their treatment
of the Fall of man in affirming the essential unity
of the race.   They represent Adam as the " root "
and " fountain head " of man.   They affirm, that
corruption of the root, involved corruption of the
branches;   and   that   pollution   of   the   fountain,

[1] "System of Christian Doctrine," trans. by Cave and Banks,
Vol. II. sec. 43.

involved pollution of the streams. Calvin says:
" We thus see that the impurity of parents is transmitted to their children, so that all, without exception, are originally depraved. The commencement
of this depravity will not be found until we ascend
to the first parent of all as the fountain head. We
must, therefore, hold it for certain, that, in regard
to human nature, Adam was not merely a progeni-
tor, but, as it were, a root, and that, accordingly,
by his corruption, the whole human race was deservedly vitiated." [1]

Davies, referring to Adam's sin, says : —

" He [God] lookes on *Adam*, as a *root*, or *well*,
    And on his heires, as *branches*, and as *streames ;*
He sees *all* men as *one* Man, though they dwell
    In sundry cities, and in sundry realmes :

" And as the *roote* and *branch* are but one *tree*,
    And *well* and *streame* doe but one *riuer* make ;
So, if the *root* and *well* corrupted bee,
    The *streame* and *branch* the same corruption take :

" So, when the root and fountaine of Mankind
    Did draw corruption, and God's curse, by sin ;
This was a charge that all his heires did bind,
    And all his offspring grew corrupt therein."

Again, with both writers, original sin means
hereditary sin. Calvin says: " Original sin, then,

[1] Op. cit., Bk. II. ch. i. sec. 6.

may be defined an hereditary corruption and depravity of our nature, extending to all the parts
of the soul, which first makes us obnoxious to the
wrath of God, and then produces in us works which
in Scripture are termed works of the flesh." [1]

Davies also affirms : —

> " So *Adam's* sinne to the whole kind extends ;
> For all their natures are but part of his."

> " Therefore this *sinne of kind*, not personall,
> But reall and hereditary was."

Again, both writers affirm that original sin involves not merely punishment for us, but also
actual guilt.   Even the child in the mother's womb
is a sinful, guilty, condemned soul.   Calvin says:
" Hence, even infants bringing their condemnation
with them from their mother's womb, suffer not for
another's, but for their own defect.   For although
they have not yet produced the fruits of their own
unrighteousness, they have the seed implanted in
them.   Nay, their whole nature is, as it were, a
seed-bed of sin, and therefore cannot but be odious
and abominable to God.   Hence it follows, that it
is properly deemed sinful in the sight of God; for
there could be no condemnation without guilt." [2]

[1] Op. cit., Bk. II. ch. i. sec. 8.
[2] Ibid.

Davies subscribes to this view of infant guilt and condemnation: —

> " And yet this *Soule* (made good by God at first,
> And not corrupted by the bodie's ill)
> Euen in the wombe is sinfull, and accurst,
> Ere shee can *iudge* by *wit* or *chuse* by *will.*"

And, again, showing how we are involved in guilt and punishment, he says: —

> " The guilt whereof, and punishment to all,
> By course of Nature, and of Law doth passe."

Still another point concerning original sin in which both writers agree is, that the soul is not only stripped of its native virtues, but that many vices take their place. On this point Calvin affirms: " After the heavenly image in man was effaced, he not only was himself punished by a withdrawal of the ornaments in which he had been arrayed, viz., wisdom, virtue, justice, truth, and holiness, and by the substitution in their place of those dire pests, blindness, impotence, vanity, impurity, and unrighteousness, but he involved his posterity also, and plunged them in the same wretchedness." [1]

[1] Op. cit., Bk. II. ch. i. sec. 5.

In similar vein Davies writes : —

> "Yet not alone the first good qualities,
>   Which in the first *soule* were, depriùed are ;
>   But in their place the contrary doe rise,
>   And reall spots of sinne her beauty marre."

Furthermore, Calvin and Davies agree in affirming that original sin in no way impeaches the justice of God. Calvin says : "That being thus perverted and corrupted in all the parts of our nature, we are, merely on account of such corruption, deservedly condemned by God, to whom nothing is acceptable but righteousness, innocence, and purity . . . The blame of our ruin rests with our own carnality, not with God, its only cause being our degeneracy from our original condition. . . . Let us remember that our ruin is attributable to our own depravity, that we may not insinuate a charge against God himself, the Author of nature. It is true that nature has received a mortal wound, but there is a great difference between a wound inflicted from without, and one inherent in our first condition. It is plain that this wound was inflicted by sin ; and, therefore, we have no ground of complaint except against ourselves." [1]

[1] Op. cit., Bk. II. ch. i. secs. 8, 10.

We have seen above how earnestly Davies insists upon the justice of God in answer to the objection of Traducianism to Creationism growing out of the doctrine of original sin. He argues that in human law offspring suffer for the crimes of parents and even of more remote ancestors, and asks : —

> " And is not God's decree as iust as ours,
>   If He, for *Adam's* sinne, his sonnes depriue,
>   Of all those natiue vertues," etc.

Finally, both writers raise the same question, or, rather, both put into the mouths of others the question as to why God did not do more to prevent Adam's fall. And, though they differ somewhat in regard to their reply, both counsel modesty with reference to prying into the mysterious and secret counsels of the Almighty. Calvin says : " And let no one here clamour that God might have provided better for our safety by preventing Adam's fall. This objection, which, from the daring presumption implied in it, is odious to every pious mind, relates to the mystery of predestination, which will afterwards be considered in its own place." [1]

[1] Op. cit., Bk. II. ch. i. sec. 10.

Davies also says : —

> "*Yet this* the curious wits will not content ;
> They yet will know (sith God foresaw this ill)
> Why His high Prouidence did not preuent
> The declination of the first man's will."

After replying to this objection in the manner already stated, he adds : —

> " Then let vs praise that Power, which makes vs be
> *Men* as we are, and rest contented so ;
> And knowing Man's fall was curiositie,
> Admire God's counsels, which we cannot know."

The number of these striking similarities in thought in the two thinkers might be increased, but a sufficient number has been pointed out to show beyond reasonable doubt that the poet was greatly influenced by the Genevan theologian in his doctrine of original sin. In meeting the objection of Traducianism against Creationism, — that it is impossible to hold the dogma of original sin and adhere to Creationism without making God responsible for the birth of each individual soul in sin, — Davies seems to have had recourse to Calvin's *Institutes* in his interpretation and application of the dogma.

CHAPTER VIII

THE RELATION OF SOUL AND BODY

THUS far our poet in his philosophy of mind has discussed the question of the reality and essential nature of mind, arguing its reality against the claims of Sensationalism and Materialism. He has explained its real nature to be that of a spiritual substance, — the fundamental modes or forms of whose functioning are intellect and will. He has also discussed the mode of the soul's origin in relation to the body, canvassing the various theories, and taking his position with the Creationists, affirming each soul to be an immediate creation on the part of the Deity, while the body is still in its pre-natal state, and vindicating the theory against the objection of Traducianism that it is inconsistent with the dogma of original sin. But if the soul be a reality, and a spiritual reality, it is nevertheless not a *disembodied* spirit. It is a spirit " knit to the body." And the next question which naturally suggests itself, and which the poet considers, is the union of soul and body. His treatment of this important question of the philosophy of mind is peculiar. Instead of attempting to explain the relation of soul and body, he first dwells upon its purpose or teleology. Then, in a subsequent part of the poem, he attempts a description of the relation. But there seems to be no effort to really explain the *ultimate nature of this relation*, which is the problem that most concerns the philosophic mind.

With reference to the object or purpose of the union of body and mind, Davies says, first, that the soul is joined to the body for the purpose of becoming a microcosm. Partaking, as it does, of the nature of God, and also, in its union with the body, of the world, it bears the image of all that is. God first created angels as pure spirits. He then created bodies or material things without spirits. He then created man —

> "th' *horizon* 'twixt both kinds,
> In whom we doe the World's abridgement see."

Just what the purpose or " final cause " of such a microcosm, as a microcosm, is, Davies fails to reveal.

Another reason why the soul was united to the body is to be found in the supposed fact, that the world needed a being who could distinguish all of its parts — making use of them, and taking delight in them. It needed a being who could order things with industry and art; a being, also, who might glorify God, admiring Him in His works, and rendering prayer and praise unto Him, as He is glorified by the angels of heaven.

Again, the irrational brute world needed a visible king to rule over it. It is in this capacity as an embodied or incarnated spirit that man has dominion over the animal world.

And, finally, the poet closes his discussion of the teleology of the union of soul and body by calling attention to the fact that it was by just such an incarnation that God united Himself to the world, so that the world might obtain everlasting bliss.

But, as already stated, the poet not only explains the teleology of the union of body and soul, but also describes it. That is, he describes the *manner* of this union. He first proceeds negatively. He tells us what the manner of the union is not. Nothing ties the soul to the body. In this respect the soul is independent of the body.

Although she moves the body, still she is not in actual contact with it. Neither does she dwell in the body as in a tent, nor as a pilot sits in his ship; nor as a spider pent in his web; nor as wax retains an impression; nor as a vessel holds water; nor as a liquor mixed in another; nor as heat in fire; nor as a voice spread in air. Not after such modes of union is the union of body and soul to be conceived. But rather after the manner of the union of the morning light with the atmosphere, which he poetically describes in these words: —

> " But as the faire and cheerfull *Morning light*,
> Doth here and there her siluer beames impart,
> And in an instant doth herselfe vnite
> To the transparent ayre, in all, and part:

> " Still resting whole, when blowes th' ayre diuide;
> Abiding pure, when th' ayre is most corrupted;
> Throughout the ayre, her beams dispersing wide,
> And when the ayre is tost, not interrupted:

> " So doth the piercing *Soule* the body fill,
> Being all in all, and all in part diffus'd;
> Indiuisible, incorruptible still,
> Not forc't, encountred, troubled or confus'd.

> " And as the *sunne* aboue, the light doth bring,
> Though we behold it in the ayre below;
> So from th' Eternall Light the *Soule* doth spring,
> Though in the body she her powers doe show."

In Davies's account of the relation between body and soul the evidence of the influence of Nemesius is very marked. There is a noticeable agreement in both thought and language. In the first place, they are in agreement in regard to the teleology of the union. According to both authors, the reason why the soul is united to the body is, the formation of a microcosm. On this point Nemesius says: " This is manifest, that MAN in some things participates with *creatures void of life ;* and that he is partaker also of *life,* as those *living-creatures* be, which are *unreasonable :* and that he is indowed likewise with *understanding,* as are *Creatures reasonable.*" [1] . . .

" These things considered, MAN standeth in such a *Being* as comprehends the *sensible* and *intelligible Nature.* In respect of his *Bodily powers,* and of his *Bodily substance* (which is subject unto *sense*) hee agrees both with *living-creatures,* and with things *void of life.* In respect of his *Reasonable part* he communicates with *Substances* which are *bodilesse* (or *spirituall*) as hath been said before." [2] . . .

" These things considered, *Moses* in expressing

----

[1] Op. cit., pp. 6–7.   [2] Ibid., pp. 8–9.

the Creation of the World, did very properly affirme that MAN was last made. Not only, because
all things being made for MAN, it was most convenient, that all such things ought first to bee
provided, which were necessarily pertinent to his
use; and that he who was to have the use of them,
should afterward be created: But, in respect both
intellectuall and *visible substances*, were created,
it seemed also convenient that *One* should be
made, by whom those two *Natures* should be so
united together, that the whole *World* might become ONE; and be in its owne selfe so agreeable, that the same might not bee at variance, or
estranged from it selfe. Even to this end, was
MAN made such a *living-creature*, as might joyne
together both *Natures*, and (to summe up all in
a word) therein was manifested the admirable
wisdome of the universall CREATOR." [1]

Again, referring to the fact that man is a microcosm, Nemesius says: " These things considered,
who is able to commend sufficiently the nobility
of this *living-creature ?* Behold, he bindeth together in *himself* things *mortall* and *immortall ;*
and knitteth up in *One*, things *reasonable* and
unreasonable. In his owne nature, hee beareth

[1] Op. cit., pp. 19–20.

the *image* of all *creatures*, and from thence is
rightly called *A little world.*" [1]

In the following words Davies also makes man
a microcosm, and says that this is the purpose of
the union of soul and body : —

> " *This substance*, and this *spirit of God's owne making*,
> Is in the body plact, and planted heere ;
> That both of God, and of the world partaking,
> Of all that is, Man might the image beare.

> " God first made angels bodilesse, pure minds,
> Then other things, which mindlesse bodies be ;
> Last, He made Man, th' *horizon* twixt both kinds,
> In whom we doe the World's abridgement see."

Thus both writers agree that one of the purposes
of the union of soul and body in man was to form
a microcosm. Not only is the thought of both
the same here, but their language is quite similar.

There are other reasons why the soul is united
to the body given by Davies, which, while not
explicitly urged by Nemesius as reasons for such
union, are nevertheless pointed out by him as the
result of man's constitution as body-mind. They
indicate further the influence of Nemesius on
Davies. Speaking of man, Nemesius says : " It
s a thing proper also, to MAN only, to learn *Arts*

---

[1] Op. cit., p. 71.

and *Sciences*, and to worke according unto such *Arts :* For which cause they who define him say thus; MAN *is a living Creature, indued with Reason, mortall, capable of Consideration and Science.*" [1] Nemesius does not say that this was part of the purpose of the union of soul and body. But it seems to be an implication of his thought that this is the result of such a constitution of man. Davies's thought and words are similar : —

> "Besides, this World below did need *one wight*,
> Which might thereof distinguish euery part ;
> Make vse thereof, and take therein delight,
> And order things with industry and art."

Again, in this connection, they agree that man is placed here to govern the brute world. Nemesius, contrasting man's constitution as body and soul with that of the angels, and also with nonrational things, points out that it is because of man's unique constitution as body-mind that he is made ruler over both the inanimate and animate worlds. Having contrasted man's nature with that of the angels, he says: "This being so, we must seek out a *Nature* which is indued with *Reason*, and yet needeth such things as are aforementioned ; and what other *nature* can be found of that sort,

[1] Op. cit., p. 47.

if MAN be passed over? Surely none: And if no other can be discovered, it followeth by good reason that both *things void of life*, and *unreasonable creatures*, were made for the sake of MAN; and if they were ordained for him (as it is evident they were) then, that was likewise the cause why he was constituted the *Governor* also of those *creatures*." [1]

Davies, also, still speaking of the reason "why the soul is united to the body," says: —

> " Lastly, the bruite, unreasonable wights,
>   Did want a *visible king* on them to raigne."

Again, in the very chapter and section referred to before in which Nemesius speaks of man as a microcosm or "little world," he not only follows with the statement, that all things were made for man, but that "He is that *creature* also, for whose sake GOD became MAN, and who shaking off his *corruption*, finisheth it in a never-ending immortality." [2]

Davies, too, still speaking of the reasons why the soul was united to the body, says: —

> " Lastly, the bruite, unreasonable wights,
>   Did want a *visible king* on them to raigne:
>   And God, Himselfe thus to the World vnites, —
>   That so the World might endlesse blisse obtaine."

[1] Op. cit., pp. 52–53.   [2] Ibid., pp. 71–72.

But we not only find a likeness in thought and language between the two writers in their discussion of the teleology of the union of soul and body, but also a striking similarity in what they say concerning the *manner* of this union. Both writers first proceed negatively in their descriptions. They make use of the method of exclusion, and then state positively what is the manner of the union of soul and body. But there is not merely an agreement in their *form* of treatment of the subject, but also in the *content*, and in the language which embodies the content.

In the first place they agree that the soul is not in the body as one material thing is in another. Nemesius argues this at some length.[1]

Davies says : —

> " Then dwels shee not therein as in a tent,
>   Nor as a pilot in his ship doth sit ;
>   Nor as the spider in his web is pent ;
>   Nor as the waxe retaines the print in it."

But Nemesius becomes more specific, and makes use of illustrations, and here, in the second place, there is an agreement between the two writers on the subject. Nemesius says, that the soul is not in the body as in a vessel or bottle. "Neither

[1] Op. cit., pp. 185–202.

is it in the *body* as in some bottle or other vessell, nor compassed in by the same." [1]

So Davies : —

> " Nor as a vessell water doth containe."

Again, Nemesius says, soul and body are not united as in a mixture of wine and water. In the latter there is " corruption and confusion " — no preservation of the distinctness of each, whereas in the union of soul and body such " corruption and confusion " do not occur. " And as for such a mixture as is made of *wine* and *water*, wee know it corrupts both the one and the other; for there doth remaine neither pure *water*, nor pure *wine*, after such a mixture." [2]

Davies says : —

> " Nor as a vessell water doth containe ;
> Nor as one liquor in another shed."

Again, Nemesius says, that the soul is not in the body as fire is in the wood. But he says this in an indirect way. He likens the relation of the soul to the body, to the relation of the sun to the air, but with this difference, " that the *Sunne* being a *Body*, and circumscribed within the compasse of *Place*, is not himselfe in every

[1] Op. cit., p. 199.   [2] Ibid., p. 189.

place where his *light* is, but (as *fire* in the *wood*, or as the *flame* in a *candle*) is confined to a certaine *place*." [1]

So Davies affirms, immediately after the lines quoted above: —

> " Nor as the heat doth in the fire remaine;
> Nor as a voice throughout the ayre is spread."

Thus both writers describe the union of soul and body negatively. But they also describe it positively or affirmatively. And in this affirmative description Davies uses the very same simile used by Nemesius. The latter says: " For, as the *Sun*, so soon as it appeareth, changes the *ayre* into *light;* so making it lightsome, and so diffusing it selfe with the *ayre*, that it is united with the same, and yet not confounded therewith: Even so, the *soul* being united with the *Body*, remaines without confusion therewith; differing in this onely, that the *Sunne* being a *Body*, and circumscribed within the compasse of *Place*, is not him selfe in every place where his *light* is, but (as *fire* in the *wood*, or as the *flame* in a *candle*) is confined to a certaine *place*." [2]

In strikingly similar language Davies describes the relation of soul and body. He says: —

[1] Op. cit., p. 198.   [2] Ibid., pp. 197–198

" But as the faire and cheerfull *Morning light*,
   Doth here and there her siluer beames impart,
   And in an instant doth herselfe vnite
   To the transparent ayre, in all, and part :

" Still resting whole, when blowes th' ayre diuide ;
   Abiding pure, when th' ayre is most corrupted ;
   Throughout the ayre, her beams dispersing wide,
   And when the ayre is tost, not interrupted :

" So doth the piercing *Soule* the body fill,
   Being all in all, and all in part diffus'd ;
   Indiuisible, incorruptible still,
   Not forc't, encountred, troubled or confus'd."

Not only does he use the same simile here that
is used by Nemesius as descriptive of the relation
between soul and body, but in the last verse of
the above quotation, he uses the same terms that
Nemesius uses in speaking of this relation. He
speaks of the " piercing soul," as " being all in
all," and " all in part," as " incorrupted " by this
union, as not " forced," " encountered," or " con-
fused." These, and others having the same meaning, abound in the description by Nemesius.[1]

It seems evident from this comparison of the descriptions of the union between soul and body by
Nemesius and Davies that the latter was influenced
decidedly by the former. And when we add this

[1] Cf. op. cit., pp. 185–202.

evidence to the evidence previously adduced in favor of the position that the poet-philosopher is indebted to the Church Father for aid, it places the matter beyond reasonable doubt.

It will be noticed that in the account of the relation between body and mind by Davies there is hardly anything beyond a mere description of their union. This seems rather remarkable in view of the degree of thoroughness with which he apprehends and treats the other problems of a philosophy or metaphysics of mind. One cannot think seriously on this problem for any length of time without perceiving that it is one of the most important, far-reaching, as well as one of the most difficult problems with which the metaphysician must deal. For, after all, the problem is but one aspect of a more general one — the problem of interaction — how one thing can act upon another. And the answer we give to this question will determine the character of our entire metaphysical system — whether it shall be dualistic or monistic, materialistic or idealistic, theistic or pantheistic. For in the final analysis, it involves the two most fundamental questions of metaphysics — the ultimate nature of reality and the relation of the finite to the Absolute. This being so, one cannot justly dismiss the problem of the relation of mind and body with a mere descriptive statement of it, as Davies has done. Davies's failure to treat the subject with philosophical thoroughness stands in glaring contrast to the serious consideration received by it in the century immediately following. In this, the seventeenth century, it was thoroughly handled, and there was a rich development of speculative opinion concerning the ultimate nature of the relation between mind and body, especially in the theories of causal relation by Descartes, of psycho-physical parallelism by Spinoza, occasionalism by Malebranche and Geulincx, and pre-established harmony by Leibnitz.

CHAPTER IX

HOW THE SOUL EXERCISES ITS POWERS IN
THE BODY

DAVIES next considers how tne mind exercises its various powers in the body. This
very naturally leads him to an analysis and description of the different powers or activities of
the soul. Here again his work is crude, but not
any more so than is the psychology of the Middle
Ages. If we remember, too, the state of physics
and physiology at that time, it will make us char-
itable in our judgment of the poet's work, especially in the treatment of the senses.

In the first place, the soul is possessed of a
vegetative or quickening power. The office or
function of this power is to vivify, animate, nourish,
and preserve the body. It is present in every
living part of the bodily organism, and serves it
as a nurse or mother.

In the second place, the soul is endowed with
the power of sense. The office of this power is

to acquaint the mind with the superficial qualities or forms of things — the colors, tastes, odors, sounds, sizes, forms, etc., of things. Not with the inner, but with the outer nature of things — with the externals. The process of sense-perception, however, is not carefully analyzed : —

> " This power, in parts made fit, fit obiects takes,
> Yet not the things, but forms of things receiues ;
> As when a seale in waxe impression makes,
> The print therein, but not it selfe it leaues."

As to the number of the soul's senses, he holds to the old Aristotelian classification — five — which he treats in the following order, — sight, hearing, taste, smelling, feeling or touch. And, first, the sense of sight.

The eyes, the organs of vision, are located in the head, and thus —

> " Stand as one watchman, spy, or sentinell."

Although two in number, they act as one — although they both see, they report but one thing. They perceive the forms of all things and all places. They serve as guides to the body. They are the chief source of information to the soul. They contribute no beams to the objects, but receive rays from them, which rays, —

> " in the *eyes* with pointed angles end."

Explaining further the physical process of vision, he says : —

" If th' obiects be farre off, the rayes doe meet
  In a sharpe point, and so things seeme but small ;
  If they be neere, their rayes doe spread and fleet,
  And make broad points, that things seeme great withall."

Finally, he mentions nine essentials for distinct vision — the power to see, the light, the visible thing, which must not be too small, or thin, or near, or far; and clear space and time. The science of optics and the art of painting are based upon the sense of sight.

He next deals with hearing. The organs of hearing are the ears. Their real office —

" is the troubled ayre to take,
  Which in their mazes formes a sound or noyse,
  Whereof her selfe doth true distinction make."

The ears are located high, —

" Because all sounds doe lightly mount aloft."

Furthermore, the ears are constructed as they are — there being no direct passage of the stimulus to the brain, — for the protection of the brain. The obstructions to an immediate striking of the brain on the part of the stimulus afforded by the tympanum and the windings and turnings between

the outer ear and the brain, save the latter from
astonishment and confusion. These "plaits and
folds" restrain the sound so that it comes with
a gentle touch to the brain. He likens this relation of the physical stimulus of sound to the
brain to the flow of winding streams: —

> "As streames, which with their winding banks doe play,
> Stopt by their creeks, run softly through the plaine;
> So in th' Eares' labyrinth the voice doth stray,
> And doth with easie motion touch the braine."

But while the sense of hearing is the slowest, it
is, on the other hand, the daintiest sense. It is
capable of very fine discriminations. The art of
music is founded on this sense. But its proper
object is human speech, and especially the speech
uttered by the heralds of God. The senses of
sight and hearing are the most informing senses.
They bring most knowledge to the soul. The
other senses, as we shall see, are more concerned
with the good and ill of the body: —

> "Thus by the organs of the *Eye* and *Eare*,
> The *Soule* with knowledge doth her selfe endue;
> Thus she her prison, may with pleasure beare,
> Hauing such prospects, all the world to view.

> "These conduit-pipes of knowledge feed the Mind,
> But th' other three attend the Body still;
> For by their seruices the *Soule* doth find,
> What things are to the body, good or ill."

The first of these body-serving senses of which
he treats is taste.   Inasmuch as the life of the
body is fed with meats and air, the soul makes
use of the sense of taste, by which —

" In veines, which through the tongue and palate spred,"

it distinguishes every relish.   This sense is primarily the body's nurse, but man also delights in
the pleasures of taste.   As a result, the art of
cooking comes into being.

The next sense to be considered is the sense of
smell.   It is located in the nostrils.   Its office is —

" To iudge all ayres, whereby we *breath* and *liue*."

We find this sense also to be " mistresse of an
Art," which deals with sweet perfumes.   This art
imparts little good, — those smelling best who
smell least.   Still, good odors purify the brain,
awaken the fancy, and refine the wits: —

" Hence old *Deuotion*, *incense* did ordaine
To make mens' spirits apt for thoughts diuine."

Lastly, the poet treats of the sense of feeling or
touch.   It is the root of life.   It is omnipresent
in the living body —

" By sinewes, which extend from head to foot,
And like a net, all ore the body spred."

Its function is to acquaint us with such qualities
of bodies as hot and cold, moist and dry, hard
and soft, rough and smooth.   Through touch
also we experience pleasure and pain.

The poet ends his account of the senses by
again calling attention to their relation to the
higher powers of mind : —

> "These are the outward instruments of Sense,
>   These are the guards which euery thing must passe
>   Ere it approch the mind's intelligence,
>   Or touch the Fantasie, *Wit's looking-glasse.*"

Having thus treated of the power of sense, he
next takes up the subject of the imagination or
common sense.   Here he enters a little more into
an explanation or description of the mechanism
involved in the apprehension of things by sense,
for in such apprehension the imagination and fantasie are concerned.   The senses themselves really
do not perceive.   They —

> " Themselues perceiue not, nor discerne the things."

There is a common power, "which doth in the
forehead sit," which brings together the forms of
external things collected by the senses.   Because
all of the nerves which spread to the outward
organs, and which bear the " spirits of sense," are

united in this portion of the brain; and here are
discerned, by a common power which is called
the imagination or the common sense, the "sundry
formes" of sense.

But now occurs another process — a transmis-
sion of these forms thus perceived by imagination
or common sense to a still higher region of the
brain, where is located another power of mind —
the "fantasie": —

> "Those outward organs present things receiue,
>   This inward *Sense* doth absent things retaine;
>   Yet straight transmits all formes shee doth perceiue,
>   Vnto a higher region of the *braine*."

This power of fantasie beholds and discerns the
forms thus transmitted; compounds and compares
them, and tests their values. It is an exceedingly
busy power, operating day and night — the flutter-
ing wings of a thousand dreams keeping it awake
when the senses are at rest.

There is still another power involved in the
apprehension of sense — the sensitive memory.
Notwithstanding the activity of the fantasie, all
forms may not be present to her sight. Those
which she has ceased to see are retained by
memory, which power is located in the rear part
of the brain. With this brief mention of the

sensitive memory we reach an end of " sense's apprehension : " —

> " Heere *Sense's apprehension*, end doth take;
> As when a stone is into water cast,
> One circle doth another circle make,
> Till the last circle touch the banke at last."

But there are also " passions of sense " which are caused in the heart by the " motiue vertue " of the soul. These passions are joy, grief, fear, hope, hate, and love. They possess " a free commanding might," and different actions are impelled by them. All actions not directed by reason spring from these passions. Now the question arises, How, if the power of sense is located in the brain, does the brain give rise to these passions of sense in the heart? It is due to the mutual love and kind intelligence which exist between the brain and heart. But more specifically it may be explained as follows: The " spirits of life " have their origin in the heat of the heart. When the " spirits of life " ascend to the brain, they give rise to the " spirits of sense." These " spirits of sense " judge of the nature of objects whether good or ill, in the court of the fantasie. They report their judgments to the heart — the seat of the passions. If the report be good, the passions

of love, hope, and joy are called into being. If
the report be ill, it causes hatred, fear, and grief.
These natural passions would be good, were reason possessed of its original perfection, so as to
properly direct them.

But there is still another motive power which
comes from the heart, —

> "from whose pure blood do spring
> The *vitall spirits;* which, borne in *arteries*,
> Continuall motion to all parts doe bring.

> " This makes the pulses beat, and lungs respire,
> This holds the sinewes like a bridle's reines;
> And makes the Body to aduance, retire,
> To turne or stop, as she them slacks, or straines.

> " Thus the *soule* tunes the *bodie's* instrument;
> These harmonies she makes with *life* and *sense;*
> The organs fit are by the body lent,
> But th' actions flow from the *Soule's* influence."

The poet now turns to the consideration of the
two powers of the soul which are really expressive
of its nature, — the powers of wit and will. These
powers are peculiar to man's soul as compared
with the animal soul. On earth no other being
is endowed with these higher powers of mind.
The poet first deals with the power of wit. This
power looks into the fantasie, wherein the senses

gather, and abstracts from thence the shapes or forms of things. These, after being received into the passive part of the wit or intellect, are enlightened by the active intellect, and thus the mind or intellect perceives the forms of single things. The next step is by discourse, anticipation, and comparison, to gain a knowledge of universal natures, and to trace effects to their causes. Now the power of wit is known by different names as it functions differently. When it reasons, or "moues from ground to ground," it is known as *reason*. When by this process of reasoning it has attained the truth, and stands fixed therein, it is known as *understanding*. When the wit only slightly assents, then it is *opinion*. When it defines a certain truth by principles, then we have *judgment*. Many reasons lead to understanding. Many understandings lead to knowledge, and much knowledge leads to wisdom. But while man thus ascends by steps to wisdom, he has a certain native power — certain "sparkes of light," by which he can discern "some common things": —

> " For Nature in man's heart her lawes doth pen ;
> Prescribing *truth* to *wit*, and *good* to *will ;*
> Which doe *accuse*, or else *excuse* all men,
> For euery thought or practise, good or ill."

" And yet these sparkes grow almost infinite,
    " Making the World, and all therein their food."

These sparks were almost quenched by the Fall of man, but they are increased by a heavenly light in those who have been justified through faith in Christ.

Now just as we are endowed with wit, which should truly *know* goodness, so we are endowed with will, which ought to *choose* true goodness. Will often errs in choosing, taking evil for good, and good for evil, simply because of the error of wit. The relations between wit and will are very intimate, and the poet points these out. Will executes what wit devises. Will acts; wit contemplates. And as wisdom arises from wit, so all other virtues spring from the will. Wit is counsellor to will, and will carries out its counsels. Wit is the chief judge of the mind, controlling the judgments of the fancy. Will is king and with its royal sceptre rules the passions of the heart. Finally, the poet affirms that will is free. The soul in the exercise of this power is neither restrained nor constrained by any outside power. It is a self-determining being: —

" *Will* is as free as any emperour,
        Naught can restraine her *gentle* libertie ;
        No tyrant, nor no torment, hath the power,
        To make vs *will*, when we vnwilling bee."

The last faculty or power with which the poet deals, is the intellectual memory. It may seem singular to follow the analysis and description of wit and will — the highest powers of the soul, — with a brief notice and description of another power. But there is a kind of logical order observed here. He has already described the sensitive memory, which is the "lidger-booke" of sense. But there is also a "lidger-booke" of wit and will — a storehouse for their products — "all arts and generall reasons." This intellectual memory is immortal. Its records survive death. No "Lethœan flood" can wash them away: —

> "To these high powers, a store-house doth pertaine,
>   Where they all arts and generall reasons lay;
>   Which in the *Soule*, euen after death, remaine,
>   And no *Lethœan* flood can wash away."

Thus a survey of the human mind reveals a diversity of powers, each one having its own proper function or office, and one exceeding "another in degree." But notwithstanding this diversity of powers — these differences in function and degree — they sustain a mutual dependence. The wit of man is given him for the purpose of knowing Almighty God. His will is given him for the purpose of loving God, being known. But the human mind could not know God save by His works, and these can only be revealed through sense. So that wit and will are dependent on sense. Again, sense in turn is dependent upon a lower power, the quickening power. This feeds or nourishes the power of sense. And so it is, as we have already seen, that the lower powers are also dependent upon the higher. And it is as men actually evaluate these powers in their living, that they are high or low in the scale of human life.

Finally, there is one more point to be noted. The three powers — sense, wit, and will, — although spoken of as powers, must not be regarded as distinct entities or agents. That is, they are not three souls. They constitute but one soul. They are three modes of the one soul's functioning —three fundamental forms of the soul's activity.

This ends the account of how the soul exercises its powers in the body, in which account Davies also presents to the reader his analysis and description of the various powers of the mind, and his conception of their mutual relations. After thus surveying the whole field of the mind's activities, he is so overcome with the marvellous constitution of man that he breaks forth with the acclamation : —

" O ! what is Man (great Maker of mankind !)
    That Thou to him so great respect dost beare !
    That Thou adornst him with so bright a mind,
    Mak'st him a king, and euen an angel's peere !

" O ! what a liuely life, what heauenly power,
    What spreading vertue, what a sparkling fire !
    How great, how plentifull, how rich a dower
    Dost Thou within this dying flesh inspire !

" Thou leau'st Thy print in other works of Thine,
    But Thy whole image Thou in Man hast writ;
    There cannot be a creature more diuine,
    Except (like Thee) it should be infinit.

" But it exceeds man's thought, to thinke how hie
    God hath raisd *Man*, since *God a man* became ;
    The angels doe admire this *Misterie*,
    And are astonisht when they view the same."

Davies's analysis of the powers of the mind
is, fundamentally considered, Aristotelian. In the
first place, with both writers the real soul of man
is independent of the body, and is distinguished
from the soul as possessing certain powers by
virtue of its connection with the body — which
forms the " animal soul " as Aristotle calls it. The
higher soul of man Aristotle calls νοῦς, and the
active νοῦς (as distinguished from the passive)
corresponds to the higher soul of man as conceived of by Davies, — the soul as possessed of

" wit and will." In discussing the relation of Reason to the other " faculties," Aristotle says: " This consideration shews how improbable it is that reason should be incorporated with the bodily organism: for if so, it would be of some definite character, either hot or cold, or it would have some organ for its operation, just as is the case with sense." . . .

" The difference, however, between the impassivity of the faculty of reason and of the faculty of sense is clear from a consideration of the organs and the processes of sense-perception. Sense, for example, is unable to acquire perception from an object which is in too great excess — cannot, to take an instance, perceive sound from extremely loud noises, nor see nor smell anything from too violent colours and odours. Reason, on the contrary, when it applies itself to something extremely intellectual, does not lessen but rather increases its power of thinking inferior objects, the explanation being that the faculty of sense is not independent of the body, whereas reason is separated from it." [1]

So Davies affirms the independence of the soul.

---

[1] Op. cit., Bk. III. ch. iv. secs. 4, 5. See also Bk. II. ch. ii. secs. 4-10.

The soul as " wit " and " will " is in a sense really
independent of the body : —

> " These actions in her closet all alone,
>   (Retir'd within her selfe) she doth fulfill ;
>   Vse of her bodie's organs she hath none,
>   When she doth vse the powers of Wit and Will."

In the second place, both writers agree in regard
to the general powers of the soul.   They are five
in number.   Aristotle says : " Of the powers of
soul which have been mentioned, some organ-
isms, as has been said, possess all, others again a
few, while a third class possesses one only.   The
powers in question are those of nutrition, of
sensation, of desire, of local movement and of
reasoning." [1]

So Davies says : —

> " And though this spirit be to the body knit,
>   As an apt meane her powers to exercise ;
>   Which are *life, motion, sense*, and *will*, and *wit*,
>   Yet she *suruiues*, although the body *dies*."

Aristotle speaks also of the powers as four in
number, evidently regarding desire and local movement as representing conation.[2]   Davies, also,
sometimes speaks of them as four ;   namely,
vegetative power, sense, wit, and will, as will be

[1] Op. cit., Bk. II. ch. iii. sec. 1.   [2] Ibid., sec. 7.

apparent in a moment in his description of the
relation of the powers.

In the third place, both writers agree in recognizing the intimate relation existing between these
powers.   Aristotle makes the lower potentially
existent in the higher.   Davies speaks of the lower
as ministering to the higher.   Aristotle says:
" The different forms of soul in fact stand to one
another in the same way as do the several species
of figure: both in the case of figures and of animate beings, the earlier form always exists potentially in the later." [1]

Davies in describing the relation of these powers
says: —

" *Our Wit* is giuen, *Almighty God* to *know;*
   Our *Will* is giuen to *loue* Him, being *knowne;*
   But God could not be *known* to vs below,
   But by His *workes* which through the sense are shown.

" And as the *Wit* doth reape the fruits of *Sense,*
   So doth the *quickning* power the *senses feed;*
   Thus while they doe their sundry gifts dispence,
   The best, the seruice of the least doth need.

" Euen so the King his Magistrates do serue,
   Yet Commons feed both magistrate and king ;
   The Commons' peace the magistrates preserue
   By borrowed power, which from the Prince doth spring.

[1] Op. cit., Bk. II. ch. iii. secs. 6, 7.

" The *quickning power* would *be,* and so would rest ;
  The *Sense* would not *be* onely, but *be well;*
  But *Wit's* ambition longeth to the *best,*
  For it desires in endlesse blisse to dwell."

In the fourth place, both writers in their analysis
of the powers of the soul are careful to emphasize
the unity of the soul.   Aristotle, although speaking sometimes of the various powers of the soul as
though they were souls, does not mean this.   He
teaches rather that they are really modes or aspects of the one soul's functioning.   This is a
fundamental implication of his teaching concerning the relation of the powers.[1]

Likewise, Davies, closing his discussion of the
relation of reason, sense, and the vegetative power,
says : —

" Yet these three powers are not three *soules,* but one;
  As one and two are both containd in *three*
  Three being one number by it selfe alone :
  A shadow of the blessed Trinitie."

In Davies's more detailed analysis of the mental
" faculties " he deviates somewhat from Aristotle.
This may be an original element introduced here,
or it may be an introduction of a small element of
contemporary psychology.

Several points worthy of note in connection

[1] Op. cit., Bk. II. ch. iii.

with Davies's analysis and description of the mental powers, pertain to his relation to Nemesius. First, the latter teaches Aristotle's doctrine of the vegetative power, or the power of nutrition, belonging to the soul. Davies, as we have seen, also recognizes this power, and his description of its method of working is so like that of Nemesius as to indicate that he was influenced by him. Nemesius says: "All the naturall faculties of the *nourishing power*, are these foure; an *attractive appetite*, a *retentive power*, a *distributing*, and an *expulsive* (or avoiding) *facultie:* for every part of the *living-creature*, doth naturally *draw* unto itselfe such nourishment, as is convenient for the same: when it is attracted, it *preserveth* it: when the same is kept a due time, it *changeth* the same into it selfe; and then *expelleth* whatsoever proveth to be superfluous." [1]

In similar language Davies describes the functioning of this power. He, too, attributes to it the offices of attracting, retaining, distributing, and expelling: —

> "*Her quick'ning* power in euery liuing part,
> Doth as a nurse, or as a mother serue ;
> And doth employ her *oeconomicke art*,
> And busie care, her household to preserue.

[1] Op. cit., pp. 397–398.

> " Here she *attracts*, and there she doth *retaine*,
>   There she *decocts*, and doth the food prepare ;
>   There she *distributes* it to euery vaine,
>   Here she *expels* what she may fitly spare."

Of course, it must be remembered that when two writers agree in regard to the functioning of a power or agent, their language must necessarily be similar. But the language and its content are so strikingly similar here as to indicate, especially in view of the evidence already presented, that Davies was influenced by Nemesius. Second, an instance similar to the above is found in the description given by both writers of the source of the " vital spirits." Nemesius says : " Because the *vitall-spirit* is dispersed from the *heart* by the *arteries*, into every part of the *body*." [1]

Davies, in discussing the " Motion of Life," in connection with his analysis of the mental powers, thinks and speaks of the vital spirits as does Nemesius : —

> " Besides, another *motiue*-power doth rise
>   Out of the heart ; from whose pure blood do spring
>   The *vitall spirits ;* which, borne in *arteries*,
>   Continuall motion to all parts doe bring."

[1] Op. cit., p. 408.

They agree in recognizing the existence of vital spirits; also in regard to their seat, their course, and their destination.

It is interesting to note also in this connection Calvin's analysis of the mental powers with which, if our view of Davies's indebtedness to Calvin be correct, he must have been familiar. It is briefly given in the following passage: " First, I admit that there are five senses, which Plato (in The-aeteto) prefers calling organs, by which all objects are brought into a common sensorium, as into a kind of receptacle: Next comes the imagi-n..tion, (*phantasie*), which distinguishes between the objects brought into the sensorium: Next, reason, to which the general power of judgment belongs: And, lastly, intellect, which contemplates with fixed and quiet look whatever reason discursively revolves. In like manner, to intellect, fancy, and reason, the three cognitive faculties of the soul, correspond three appetitive faculties, viz., will, whose office is to choose whatever reason and intellect propounds; irascibility, which seizes on what is set before it by reason and fancy; and concupiscence, which lays hold of the objects presented by sense and fancy."[1]

[1] Op. cit., Bk. I. ch. xv. sec. 6.

There is, of course, only a general correspondence between Davies's analysis of the various "faculties" of the soul and Calvin's, which would hardly indicate anything with reference to Calvin's influence upon Davies. But in Davies's account of the function of reason in the determination of truth and goodness, and the handicap under which she labors by virtue of man's Fall; and also in his account of the relation between reason and will as that of Ruler and Guide, there is much that indicates the influence of Calvin.[1]

As indicating the position which Davies's twofold division of the powers of the real soul of man as "wit and will" holds in the history of psychology the following brief statement by Sully is substantially true, — only we can hardly say that the threefold division has been "fixed as the permanent one": "The first essay in distinguishing between co-ordinate mental functions led to a bipartite or dichotomus division, *viz.*, into an intellective and an active or conative factor. The germ of this bisectional view may be found in Aristotle, who, while he gave independent functional value to intellect or thought (νοῦς) and

[1] Cf. Calvin, op. cit., Bk. I. ch. xv. secs. 6–8; also Bk. II. ch. ii. secs. 12–26.

to desire or appetite (ὄρεξις), subordinated feeling to these. This twofold scheme remained the prevailing one up to comparatively recent times. It survives in the classification of Reid, *viz.*, (1) Intellectual and (2) Active Powers, and in the popular psychology of everyday life. The separate recognition of feeling as a co-ordinate phase or function of mind is due to the German psychologists of the Wolffian school who wrote about the middle of the last century, more especially Moses Mendelssohn and Tetens. The tripartite division was adopted from these by Kant, and by his authority fixed as the permanent one. " [1]

[1] " The Human Mind." New York, 1892, Vol. II., Appendix A. p. 327.

CHAPTER X

IMMORTALITY OF THE SOUL

HAVING covered so much of the territory of the philosophy of mind, there still remains another portion to be traversed. The poet has considered the problems of the *Whence* and the *What* of mind; he must now consider the *Whither*. He has attempted to determine its origin and nature; he must now determine, if possible, its destiny. Is the mind a mere creature of time, or does it bear the impress of eternity? In our poet's judgment the soul is immortal, and he proceeds, in the most formal manner, to give reasons for the faith within him on this most important question.

Referring to the wonderful powers of mind revealed by his psychological analysis, he says: —

> " Nor hath He giuen these blessings for a day,
> Nor made them on the bodie's life depend ;
> The *Soule* though made in time, *suruives for aye*,
> And though it hath beginning, sees no end.

> " Her only *end*, is *neuer-ending* blisse ;
>   Which is, *th' eternall face of God to see ;*
>   Who *Last of Ends*, and *First of Causes*, is :
>   And to doe this, she must *eternall* bee."

This eternity of the soul will be manifest to any one who will patiently study its nature. In its very constitution, and in some of its fundamental modes of behavior, he will discern its immortality.

Having thus stated his thesis, and hinted at the method of procedure by which it is to be established, he presents the ground for its acceptance in the form of a series of "Reasons" : —

Reason I., is based on man's desire for knowledge — a desire to "*know the truth* of euery thing" — which is native to the human soul. It is co-natural with the soul, — to use the poet's own expression. It is born with it, and springs from its very essence. Going with this native desire to know, is also a native might to discover the truth of everything, were sufficient time allowed to the soul. But this mortal life is too short for the accomplishment of such a task. Our little life passes away as rapidly —

> " As doth a hungry eagle through the wind,
>   Or as a ship transported with the tide."

So much of this short time is engaged with the few things revealed by sense, as to be really at an end —

> " Ere we the principles of skill attaine."

Here we hardly attain more than the alphabet of knowledge. Now God, who creates nothing in vain, has either given us this native appetite for perfect knowledge in vain, or our knowledge is to be perfected in another life. God never gave a power to an entire species but that the majority of the species made use of such power. But it is not so with the human species. He has endowed it with a native desire and might to know the truth perfectly, but not one member of the species can in this mortal life thus know the truth. Hence we must conclude with reference to the soul's knowledge, that if —

> "perfection be not found below,
> An higher place must make her mount thereto.'

Reason II., is based on what the poet calls the motion of the soul. The soul with its powers of wit and will aspires to eternity. Since it aspires to the eternal God, it must be an eternal thing. All moving things move toward their kind. The river, whose water was first derived from the sea, ultimately, after moving here and there, by various windings through the land, again moves toward the sea. And thus it is with the soul of man. It comes from God. It pursues earthly things. It moves here and there, seeking contentment among things temporal. But it is not satisfied with what it finds and turns to things eternal: —

" Then as a *bee* which among weeds doth fall,
    Which seeme sweet flowers, with lustre fresh and gay;
    She lights on that, and this, and tasteth all,
    But pleasd with none, doth rise, and soare away;

" So, when the *Soule* finds here no true content,
    And, like *Noah's* doue, can no sure footing take;
    She doth returne from whence she first was sent,
    And flies to *Him* that first her wings did make."

That man thus moves towards God, and is thus like God in his Eternity, is manifest in the movements of his reason and will. The rational nature of man seeks truth. It ascends from cause to cause, and does not rest until it reaches the First Cause. It is so also with will. It seeks the Good. In its pursuit of the same it finds many subordinate ends or goods. But these do not satisfy. The will cannot rest in them. It seeks a supreme good, a *summum bonum*. Now God is the Ultimate Truth or First Cause; and He is also the

Ultimate End or Supreme Good. He is the Alpha to reason, and the Omega to will. In this movement of the soul, in its two fundamental modes of action, it betrays its heavenly origin and destiny.

Reason III., is based on the contempt for death manifested by superior souls. Such souls desire the satisfactions of the immortal life, and they often experience contempt for the death of the body. This is really due to the immortal nature of the soul. For, if the death of the body involved the soul's destruction, it would mean that death is the enemy of the soul, — that is, against its essential nature. And were this so, all souls would flee from death. For the soul, like all things, is taught by its nature the lesson of self-preservation. The instinct of self-preservation, under such circumstances, would lead all souls to avoid death as far as possible. This being so, the choice spirits of the world could not err so far as to prefer honor to life : —

"For what is praise to things that nothing bee ? "

Furthermore, were the life of the soul dependent upon the body, then the soul would only seek the body's good. There would be no sacrifice of physical or bodily good for higher ends : —

> " We should not find her half so braue and bold,
>   To leade it to the Warres and to the seas ;
>   To make it suffer watchings, hunger, cold,
>   When it might feed with plenty, rest with ease."

Reason IV., is founded on the fear of death in wicked souls. Such fear proves the immortal nature of him who experiences it. For it is not annihilation that such souls fear. Rather would they welcome this. But it is, as Hamlet put it, —

> "the dread of something after death
>   . . .   puzzles the will.
>
> .   .   .   .
> Thus conscience does make cowards of us all."

Now this testimony of both good and evil souls to the soul's immortality, as explained above, is, according to the poet, Nature's testimony ; —

> "*Nature's speech*,
> Which, like *God's* Oracle, can neuer lie."

Reason V., is based on the general desire for immortality. Davies holds the position, that the desire for immortality is instinctive with man. Such a universal desire cannot be in vain, for Nature does not covet impossibilities. Fond thoughts, of course, may be cherished by some idle brain, which do not involve reality : —

> " But one *assent* of all, is euer wise."

So universal a desire as this must involve a reality
to satisfy it. From this desire springs the progress of the race—"that generall care and study,"—

> " That *launching* and *progression of the mind;*
> Which all men haue so much, of future things,
> That they no ioy doe in the present find."

From this desire for immortality also springs
man's desire for gaining surviving fame, —

> " By *tombes*, by *bookes*, by memorable *deeds*."

From it also springs the care for posterity which
characterizes man—

> " For things their kind would euerlasting make."

Hence old men plant trees the fruit of which is
to be enjoyed by another age.

If we reflect upon these things, and apply them
to ourselves, we shall find that they are Nature's
true notes of immortality.

Reason VI., is based upon the fact of doubt
and dispute concerning immortality. To doubt
immortality shows that we know immortal things.
To reason about immortality would be impossible
were man merely mortal. To judge of immortal
things involves the immortal nature of the judging
mind : —

" For when we iudge, our minds we mirrors make :
 And as those glasses which materiall bee,
 Formes of materiall things doe onely take,
 For *thoughts* or *minds* in them we cannot see;

"So, when we God and angels do conceiue,
 And thinke of *truth*, which is eternall too ;
 Then doe our minds immortall formes receiue,
 Which if they mortall were, they could not doo."

If animals were to conceive what reason is, they would necessarily have to be rational beings. So it is with the soul. If she can reason about immortality she must be immortal. So that —

" Shee proofes of her eternitie doth bring,
 Euen when she striues the contrary to proue."

The poet concludes, that even this very thought of immortality is an act of the self-moving mind, framed by the mind without the aid of the body, and, in the spirit of Plato in the *Phædrus*, he affirms that this independence of mind is evidence that she can survive the death of the body. And as a self-moving being, her motion must be everlasting, for she can never forsake herself.

But some misgivings may still arise. Although the soul may be free from any corruption springing from herself, may there not be some external cause, designed by Fate, that ultimately will de-

stroy her? So that the poet considers these misgivings and gives reply.

In the first place, perhaps the cause of the soul
itself may cease, and then the soul must die. Not
so, says the poet. For God is her Cause, and
His Word was her Maker, and this shall stand
forever — when heaven and earth shall pass like
a shadow.

But there may be something strongly antipa-
thetic to the soul that shall ultimately destroy her.
But how can there be such a contrary to the
soul —

> " Which holds all *contraries* in concord still ?

> " She lodgeth heat, and cold, and moist, and dry,
>   And life, and death, and peace, and war together;
>   Ten thousand fighting things in her doe lye,
>   Yet neither troubleth, or disturbeth either."

Still, it may be urged, she may die for want of
food. Not so, says the poet. Not only all things,
but the Eternal God himself, as well as Eternal
Truth, constitute her food.

Perhaps, however, violence can destroy her, as
" *sun-beames* dim the sight," or as a thunder-clap
or noise of cannon affects the ear. No, says the
poet, on the contrary, the soul is perfected by
encountering "things most excellent and high."

Furthermore, the soul is so subtle as to glide safely through all dangers; and the will is so free as not to abide any force.

But, after all, may not Time, the great destroyer of things, destroy the soul? No, says the poet, Time only cherishes her and increases her might. Time gives perfection to the soul, and adds new lustre to her beauty, and makes her to dwell in eternal youth. The more the soul lives, "the more she feeds on *Truth*," and the more she thus feeds, the more strength she derives; and strength is the effect of youth, which if nursed by Time, how can it cease? The poet's reply to this misgiving, which grows out of the consciousness of the destructive nature of Time, is eloquent almost to the point of sublimity: —

> " *But lastly*, *Time* perhaps at last hath power
>   To spend her liuely powers, and quench her light;
>   But old god *Saturne* which doth all deuoure,
>   Doth cherish her, and still augment her might.

> " Heauen waxeth old, and all the *spheres* aboue
>   Shall one day faint, and their swift motion stay;
>   And *Time* it selfe in time shall cease to moue;
>   *Onely the Soule suruiues*, and liues for aye.

> " Our Bodies, euery footstep that they make,
>   March towards death, vntill at last they die;
>   Whether we worke, or play, or sleepe, or wake,
>   Our life doth passe, and with *Time's* wings doth flie:

" But to the *Soule* Time doth perfection giue,
    And ads fresh lustre to her beauty still;
    And makes her in eternall youth to liue,
    Like her which nectar to the gods doth fill.

" The more she liues, the more she feeds on *Truth;*
    The more she feeds, her *strength* doth more increase:
    And what is *strength*, but an effect of *youth ?*
    Which if *Time* nurse, how can it euer cease ? "

Thus far Davies, in his reflection upon the immortality of the soul, has considered the grounds for belief in immortality, and also several misgivings which may arise even in the face of this rational evidence. But he feels that his treatment of this subject would be inadequate, did he not consider certain objections which may be urged against his position. In the consideration of these objections he proceeds as formally as before, stating first the objection candidly and clearly, and then following in a formal manner with his answer. In his answer he endeavors not only to refute the objection, but also to strengthen the arguments previously presented by him in favor of belief.

Objection I., is based on the fact that the soul grows old. This is manifest in the dotage of old men; and in the sottishness, dulness, and coldness of their brains. It is based further on the fact that the soul itself seems to be corrupted, which is evident in idiocy and insanity.

To this objection the poet replies, that it constitutes a subtle argument to those who identify sense and reason, and fail to distinguish agent from instrument, and the working power from the work. But to those who distinguish between sense and reason, and understand the relations between them, both idiocy and dotage are explicable in a manner which does not involve the integrity of the soul. As has been previously explained, there is a kind of dependence of reason upon sense in our knowledge of things. The soul united to the body is dependent upon sense for its materials, and if the region of the brain, where both the outward sense and the inward sense of fantasie are localized, be wanting in integrity, so as to fail to report things; or, reporting them, report them incorrectly, then, of course, the soul is either blind or misled. This explains idiocy. The trouble is not with the mind of the idiot. It is capable of knowing the truth and choosing the good when these are properly presented by sense and fantasie. The difficulty lies in the fact that —

> " that region of the tender braine,
> Where th' inward sense of Fantasie should sit,
> And the outward senses gatherings should retain,"

has either —

> " By Nature, or by chance, become vnfit "

to perform its office. Remove this trouble; re-
store the integrity of this "region of the tender
braine,"—

> "Then shall the *Wit*, which never had disease,
> Discourse, and iudge discreetly, as it ought."

The defect then is in the organs of sense, and not
in the soul; in the instrument, and not in the
agent; and—

> "We must not blame *Apollo*, but his lute,
> If false accords from her false strings be sent."

Dotage may be explained in a similar manner.
The trouble is not with the dotard's soul, but with
his power of sense, which has been so weakened
by age that it —

> "Cannot the prints of outward things retaine."

The soul, therefore, sits idle. This is what we
call childishness and dotage. But, were the old
man possessed of the young man's power of sense,
there would be a different result. The soul would
then function properly. Dotage, then, must not be
regarded as a weakness of the mind, but rather a
weakness of sense. If it were a waste of the former, it would be found in all old men. But such
is not the case. The majority of them, despite
the gradually wasting body, retain a quicker and

stronger mind, and a better use of their understanding, than when they were possessed of the
bodily power of youth.

Objection II., is based on the supposition, that
if the soul's organs die she will not be able to use
her powers. Such inability to use her powers
practically amounts to their extinction. Deprived
of her powers, what then is the soul? Everything is possessed of power, and acts spring from
powers. Destroy the powers and acts, and you
destroy the thing.

To this objection Davies makes reply: It is
undoubtedly true that death destroys " the instruments of sense and life," although the root of
these remain in the substance of the soul. But
just as wit and will, during the mind's union with
the body, can judge and choose without its aid,
though using the materials which are derived by
means of the body's organs, so, after the body's
destruction and the extinction of sense, the soul —

> " can discourse of what she learn'd before,
> In heaunly contemplations, all alone."

That is, the soul after the death of the body can
exercise her fundamental powers on what she
acquired during her union with the body. To this
statement Davies adds another, based undoubtedly

on belief in the resurrection of the body. He says, that ultimately these organs of sense which are destroyed by death will be revived with the revival of the body, and will perform or fulfil their wonted office. And this leads to another objection.

Objection III., involves the question as to how, in the interim, — between death and the resurrection, — the soul is to employ herself. With her power of sense gone, she can enjoy what she has previously acquired and retained through her relation with sense, —

"But she hath meanes to vnderstand no more."

And what about those poor souls who really acquire nothing through sense, and those who acquire but do not retain? Such souls, for lack of exercise, must sleep.

To this objection the poet replies by asking, why man should not have other means of knowing after death, just as children after birth feed by different means than in the pre-natal state? Could they in their mother's womb hear from her that shortly they would leave their native home, they would fear birth as much as we fear death. They would raise the question as to how they were to

be nourished in this new world. But could some
one reply to their question by informing them of
the wonders of sense that will greet them in their
new habitat, and of the "ten thousand dainties"
that will give pleasure to the sense of taste, and
nourish the body and cause it to grow, they would
regard such a statement as fabulous. Yet they
find this to be true after birth. It is the same
with the soul of man; for death is merely the
birth of the soul. Ten thousand things await its
birth, a knowledge of which, by some unknown
method, is to be acquired: —

> " So, when the *Soule* is borne (for Death is nought
>   But the *Soule's* birth, and so we should it call)
> Ten thousand things she sees beyond her thought,
>   And in an vnknowne manner knowes them all.

> " Then doth she see by spectacles no more,
>   She heares not by report of double spies ;
> Her selfe in instants doth all things explore,
>   For each thing present, and before her, lies." [1]

Objection IV., consists of the old, stereotyped
question, Why, if the soul survive death, do not

[1] Does not Davies contradict himself in thus eliminating the
work of sense from the soul's knowledge after death? For he
has previously stated with reference to the organs of sense : —

> " Yet with the body they shall all reuiue,
>   And all their wonted offices fulfill."

departed spirits return, and give us news of that
mysterious world beyond the grave? As Robert
Blair puts it in his poem entitled *The Grave :* —

> " Tell us, ye dead, will none of you in pity,
>   To those you left behind, disclose the secret?
>   Oh! that some courteous ghost would blab it out;
>   What 'tis you are, and we must shortly be." [1]

Davies in reply to this objection wants to know
why, if we believe that men live —

> " Vnder the *Zenith* of both frozen *Poles*,"

although none of them come to give us information, we cannot exercise a like faith concerning
the destiny of our souls. At death the soul is
done with earth. It has no more business here
than we have in our mother's womb. And, although all children have come from thence, what
child desires to return? This failure of departed
souls to return to earth shows that they have
reached a goodly dwelling place. And, doubtless, souls who have stood in the presence of their
Maker, look with scorn and contempt on this vile
world. And those condemned to hell, probably
for shame, or because of impossibility, do not
return.

[1] Quoted from Grosart's ed. of *Nosce Teipsum.*

Objection V., urges that politic men have spread this lie of heaven and hell as the destiny of good and evil souls to make men virtuous.

The poet answers, that those who urge this objection concede the value of virtue, and asks whether they have no other way of preserving virtue than by lying. It is not virtue and false-hood, but rather virtue and truth which best agree, and he draws the conclusion, that since the effects of this doctrine of the soul's destiny are con-fessedly so good, and virtue and truth are ever in agreement, it must be true: —

> " For, as the deuill father is of lies,
>> So vice and mischiefe doe his lyes ensue;
>> Then this good doctrine did not he deuise,
>> But made this *lye*, which saith it is not true."

Davies, in the further consideration of this objection, again falls back on the *consensus gen-tium* — " the general consent of all." How can that be false which is universally conceded or affirmed? —

> " This rich *Assyrian* drugge growes euery where;
>> As common in the *North*, as in the *East;*
>> This doctrine does not enter by the *eare*,
>> But of it selfe is natiue in the breast."

Belief in immortality is essentially a universal phenomenon. It is native to the human soul.

No one, says our poet, who believes in God, or in divine providence, doubts it. It is the root of all religion, and no nation is without a religion. Any view to the contrary impeaches the wisdom and goodness of God. And he closes the discussion of the soul's immortality by reaffirming his belief: —

> "But blest be that *Great Power*, that hath vs blest
> With longer life then Heauen or Earth can haue
> Which hath infus'd into our mortall breast
> Immortal powers, not subiect to the graue.

> "For though the Soule doe seeme her graue to beare,
> And in this world is almost buried quick;
> We haue no cause the bodie's death to feare,
> For when the shell is broke, out comes a chick." [1]

There is one more subject which the poet briefly touches upon before he closes his reflective study of the human mind. He affirms that there are three kinds of life which answer to the three essential powers of the soul. These three essential powers are, the quickening power, the power of sense, and the power of reason. There are three kinds of life which are designed to perfect

[1] Tennyson, arguing in favor of belief in immortality, in *The Ancient Sage*, says: —

"The shell must break before the bird can fly."

these powers of the soul. The first life is the pre-
natal life. Here the soul's quickening power is
engaged in nursing the body. When nourishment
becomes defective, the soul "expels her body"
and views the world. This is what we call birth.
Could the child speak, he would call it death.

Now the individual enters upon the second life
answering to the second power of the soul — the
life of sense. He enters a world —

> "Where all his *Senses* in perfection bee;
>   Where he finds flowers to smell, and fruits to taste;
>   And sounds to heare, and sundry formes to see."

After the individual has spent some time living
this life of sense, he enters upon the rational life,
which, as we have seen before, is lived in connection with the life of sense. But the rational life
does not reach its perfection here. We have here
only the dawn of reason — not the noon-day.
Reason merely awakes a little; she does not awake
to a full exercise of her power. But when the soul
quits the body at death, then she enters into a
perfect exercise. And this is the third life, and —

> "In this third life, Reason will be so bright,
>   As that her sparke will like the *sun-beames* shine;
>   And shall of God enioy the reall sight.
>   Being still increast by influence diuine."

In Davies's discussion of the soul's immortality we can easily trace the influence of Aristotle, Cicero, and Calvin. Especially is the influence of Cicero and Calvin manifest. In the second reason for belief in the soul's immortality which Davies presents, it is evident that he learned of Calvin. It is based on the "motion" of the soul, or the soul's capacity to reach God through reason and the moral will. On this subject, Calvin says: "Moreover, there can be no question that man consists of a body and a soul; meaning by soul, an immortal though created essence, which is his nobler part. Sometimes he is called a spirit. . . . It is true, indeed, that men cleaving too much to the earth are dull of apprehension, nay, being alienated from the Father of Lights, are so immersed in darkness as to imagine that they will not survive the grave; still the light is not so completely quenched in darkness that all sense of immortality is lost. Conscience, which, distinguishing between good and evil, responds to the judgment of God, is an undoubted sign of an immortal spirit. How could motion devoid of essence penetrate to the judgment-seat of God, and under a sense of guilt strike itself with terror? The body cannot be affected by any fear of spiritual punishment. This is competent only to the soul, which must therefore be endued with essence. Then the mere knowledge of a God sufficiently proves that souls which rise higher than the world must be immortal, it being impossible that any evanescent vigour could reach the very fountain of life. In fine, while the many noble faculties with which the human mind is endued proclaim that something divine is engraven on it, they are so many evidences of an immortal essence. For such sense as the lower animals possess goes not beyond the body, or at least not beyond the objects actually presented to it. But the swiftness with which the human mind glances from heaven to earth, scans the secrets of nature, and, after it has embraced all ages, with intellect and memory digests each in its proper order, and reads the future in the past, clearly demonstrates that there lurks in man a something separated from the body. We have intellect by which we are able to conceive of the invisible God and angels — a thing of which body is altogether incapable. We have ideas of rectitude, justice, and honesty — ideas which the bodily senses cannot reach. The seat of these ideas must therefore be a spirit." [1]

[1] Op. cit., Bk. I. ch. xv. sec. 2.

Davies takes essentially the same position in the following words: —

> " *Againe* how can shee but immortall bee?
>   When with the motions of both *Will* and *Wit*,
>   She still aspireth to eternitie,
>   And neuer rests, till she attaine to it?

> . . . . . .

> " *Wit*, seeking *Truth*, from cause to cause ascends,
>   And neuer rests, till it the *first* attaine;
>   *Will*, seeking *Good*, finds many middle ends,
>   But neuer stayes, till it the *last* doe gaine.

> " Now God, the *Truth*, and *First of Causes* is:
>   God is the *Last Good End*, which lasteth still;
>   Being *Alpha* and *Omega* nam'd for this;
>   *Alpha* to *Wit*, *Omega* to the *Will*.

> " Sith then her heauenly kind shee doth bewray,
>   In that to God she doth directly moue;
>   And on no mortall thing can make her stay,
>   She cannot be from hence, but from *aboue*."

Reasons III. and IV., which Davies offers as indicating the soul's immortality, based respectively on the contempt for death which good souls show, and the fear of death which wicked souls evince, are undoubtedly an implication of Christian teaching with reference to the future life of reward and punishment, — the doctrine of heaven and hell. Still Davies pronounces this contempt on the one

hand, and fear on the other, to be " Nature's
speech " : —

> " If then all *Soules*, both good and bad, doe teach,
>   With generall voice, that *soules* can neuer die,
>   'Tis not man's flattering glosse, but *Nature's speech*,
>   Which, like *God's* Oracle, can neuer lie."

We note here the influence of Cicero. In his
remarks " On the Contempt of Death," in the
Disputationes Tusculanæ, he gives reasons why the
good man, or the superior soul, should not fear
death, and points out the destiny of wicked souls.
He quotes with admiration Socrates's famous
speech before his judges, in regard to the good
man having no need to fear death. In this book
Cicero also speaks of the improbability of cour-
ageous sacrifice, were men not immortal, or were
men not possessed of belief in immortality:
" What will you say?   What do you imagine that
so many and such great men of our republic, who
have sacrificed their lives for its good, expected?
Do you believe that they thought that their names
should not continue beyond their lives?   None
ever encountered death for their country but under
a firm persuasion of immortality!   Themistocles
might have lived at his ease; so might Epami-
nondas; and, not to look abroad and among the

ancients for instance, so might I myself. But, somehow or other, there clings to our minds a certain presage of future ages; and this both exists most firmly, and appears most clearly, in men of the loftiest genius and greatest souls. Take away this, and who would be so mad as to spend his life amidst toils and dangers? I speak of those in power. What are the poet's views but to be ennobled after death? What else is the object of these lines,

> Behold old Ennius here, who erst
> Thy fathers' great exploits rehearsed?

He is challenging the reward of glory from those men whose ancestors he himself had ennobled by his poetry. And in the same spirit he says, in another passage,

> Let none with tears my funeral grace, for I
> Claim from my works an immortality.

Why do I mention poets? The very mechanics are desirous of fame after death. Why did Phidias include a likeness of himself in the shield of Minerva, when he was not allowed to inscribe his name on it? What do our philosophers think on the subject? Do not they put their names to those very books which they write on the contempt of glory? If, then, universal consent is the voice of nature, and if it is the general opinion everywhere that those who have quitted this life are still interested in something, we also must subscribe to that opinion. And if we think that men of the greatest abilities and virtues see most clearly into the power of nature, because they themselves are her most perfect work, it is very probable that, as every great man is especially anxious to benefit posterity, there is something of which he himself will be sensible after death." [1]

Compare with these words the following words of Davies: —

> " For all things else, which Nature makes to bee,
>   Their *being* to preserue, are chiefly taught;
>   And though some things desire a change to see,
>   Yet neuer thing did long to turne to naught.

> " If then by death the *soule* were quenchèd quite,
>   She could not thus against her nature runne;
>   Since euery senselesse thing, by Nature's light,
>   Doth preservation seeke, destruction shunne.

> " Nor could the World's best spirits so much erre,
>   If death tooke all — that they should all agree,
>   Before this life, their *honour* to preferre;
>   For what is praise to things that nothing bee?

[1] Op. cit., Bk. I. sec. 15. All quotations from Cicero are from Yonge's translation, New York, 1877.

" Againe, if by the bodie's prop she stand;
   If on the bodie's life, her life depend;
   As *Meleager's* on the fatall brand, —
   The bodie's good shee onely would intend:

" We should not find her half so braue and bold,
   To leade it to the Warres and to the seas;
   To make it suffer watchings, hunger, cold,
   When it might feed with plenty, rest with ease.

" Doubtlesse all *Soules* have a suruiuing thought;
   Therefore of death we thinke with quiet mind;
   But if we thinke of *being turn'd to nought*,
   A trembling horror in our *soules* we find."

In Davies's fifth reason for affirming the immortality of the soul, we note again the influence of Cicero upon his thinking. Under " Reason V." he really includes a number of reasons, all of which are to be found in Cicero. We have the universal desire or general assent to the belief; also the " launching " of the mind into future things. We have the desire for posthumous fame springing out of the desire for immortality. We have also care for posterity arising from this desire. A comparison of the views and language of the two authors will leave no doubt as to Davies's obligation to Cicero. Cicero, after a long discussion of the argument from general assent, says: " But as we are led by nature to think there are Gods, and as we discover, by reason, of what description they are, so, by the consent of all nations, we are induced to believe that our souls survive." [1]

And, again, in language which Davies closely follows: "But the greatest proof of all is, that nature herself gives a silent judgment in favor of the immortality of the soul, inasmuch as all are anxious, and that to a great degree, about the things which concern futurity:

> One plants what future ages shall enjoy,

as Statius saith in his Synephebi. What is his object in doing so, except that he is interested in posterity? Shall the industrious husbandman, then, plant trees the fruit of which he shall never see? And shall not the great man found laws, institutions, and a republic? What does the procreation of children imply, and our care to continue our names, and our adoptions, and our scrupulous exactness in drawing up wills, and the inscriptions on monuments, and panegyrics, but that our thoughts run on futurity? There is no doubt but a judgment may be formed of nature in general, from looking at each nature in its most perfect specimens; and what is a more perfect

[1] Op. cit., Bk. I. sec. 16.

specimen of a man than those are who look on themselves as born for the assistance, the protection, and the preservation of others? Hercules has gone to heaven; he never would have gone thither had he not, while among men, made that road for himself. These things are of old date, and have, besides, the sanction of universal religion." [1]

So Davies says: —

" *Hence springs* that vniuersall strong desire,
   Which all men haue of Immortalitie :
   Not some few spirits vnto this thought aspire ;
   But all mens' minds in this vnited be.

" Then this desire of Nature is not vaine,
   She couets not impossibilities ;
   Fond thoughts may fall into some idle braine,
   But one *assent* of all, is euer wise.

" From hence that generall care and study springs,
   That *launching* and *progression of the mind ;*
   Which all men haue so much, of future things,
   That they no ioy doe in the present find.

" From this desire, that maine desire proceeds,
   Which all men haue suruiuing Fame to gaine ;
   By *tombes*, by *bookes*, by memorable *deeds :*
   For she that this desires, doth still remaine.

" Hence lastly, springs care of posterities,
   For things their kind would euerlasting make ;
   Hence is it that old men do plant young trees,
   The fruit whereof another age shall take.

[1] Op. cit., Bk. I. sec. 14.

"If we these rules vnto our selues apply,
　　And view them by reflection of the mind;
　　All these true notes of immortalitie
　　In our *heart's tables* we shall written find."

Reason VI., based on the "Doubt and Dispu-
tation of Immortalitie," is simply another way of
stating Calvin's argument; namely, that the fact
that we can form ideas of immortal things is evidence of our immortality.　Davies affirms, that to
doubt immortality is to reveal an idea of "immortal things," and thus to reveal the doubter's immortal nature.　Calvin puts the argument thus:
"We have intellect by which we are able to conceive of the invisible God and angels — a thing of
which body is altogether incapable.　We have
ideas of rectitude, justice, and honesty — ideas
which the bodily senses cannot reach.　The seat
of these ideas must therefore be a spirit."[1]　And
the context shows that he uses spirit in this connection as synonymous with immortal spirit.　For
he says: "Moreover, there can be no question
that man consists of a body and a soul; meaning by soul, an immortal though created essence,
which is his nobler part.　Sometimes he is called
a spirit."[2]

[1] Op. cit., Bk. I. ch. xv. sec. 2.　　　　[2] Ibid.

Davies, in speaking of the idea of " immortal things " involved in the sceptic's denial of immortality, says : —

> "So, when we God and angels do conceiue,
>   And thinke of *truth*, which is eternall too;
>   Then doe our minds immortall formes receiue,
>   Which if they mortall were, they could not doo."

Cicero and Calvin, then, constitute the chief sources of influence upon Davies's thinking on the subject of the immortality of the soul.   But there is a general argument underlying Davies's entire thought on this subject for which, as we have seen, he is indebted primarily to Aristotle; namely, the soul's independence of the body.

The subject of immortality has figured conspicuously in the history of speculative thought. The preponderance of speculative opinion has been favorable to the belief.   Early in the history of Greek philosophy it was held by the Pythagoreans.   It is involved in their doctrine of metempsychosis or transmigration of souls.

If we are justified in assuming that the words put into the mouth of Socrates in the *Phædo* by Plato are representative of the views of Socrates on immortality, then Socrates was undoubtedly

14

an able champion of the belief. And there seems no reason for doubting the above assumption.

Plato, as has already been suggested, argues at length in the *Phædo* the reality of immortality. So numerous and varied are his arguments that one's surprise increases as he reflects upon Davies's failure to interrogate Plato on this question in which the poet was so deeply interested.[1]

It is sometimes disputed whether Aristotle believed in the immortality of the soul. In trying to answer the question it is of importance to keep in mind the distinction which he makes between the animal soul—the soul as connected with the body—and the active $\nu o\hat{\nu}\varsigma$ or the Reason,—the soul whose essential existence is independent of the body. If we keep this distinction in mind it cannot be doubted that Aristotle teaches the immortality of the active $\nu o\hat{\nu}\varsigma$ or Reason. On this point he says: —

"Reason however would seem to constitute a different phase of soul from those we have already noticed and it alone admits of separation as the eternal from the perishable."[2] And again: —

---

[1] Except in one instance indirectly through Cicero.
[2] Op. cit., Bk. II. ch. ii. sec. 10.

" Further, this creative reason does not at one time think, at another time not think: (it thinks eternally:) and when separated from the body it remains nothing but what it essentially is: and thus it is alone immortal and eternal." [1]

It is impossible here to enter into the controversy as to whether Aristotle's doctrine of immortality involves a personal immortality or not.[2] Our own opinion is, that while he does not explicitly teach a personal immortality, his doctrine of Reason or active *νοῦς* is not inconsistent with such a view.

After Aristotle, probably the most conspicuous advocate of the reality of immortality in Greek and Græco-Roman thought, was Cicero. His views have already been given.

Of course the doctrine of a personal immortality is pre-eminently a Christian doctrine. It is not only taught in the New Testament, but Christian speculative thought practically from its beginning down to the present day has affirmed either the essential immortality of the soul, or an acquired immortality.

[1] Op. cit., Bk. III. ch. v. sec. 2.

[2] Cf. Zeller, "Aristotle and the Earlier Peripatetics," Eng. trans. London, 1897, Vol. II. pp. 129–135; also Janet and Séailles, "History of the Problems of Philosophy," trans. by Monahan. London, 1902, Vol. II. pp. 355–359.

Probably the most conspicuous representatives of the doctrine of a *personal* immortality in Modern Philosophy are Leibnitz and Kant. The former founds his belief on a doctrine of development which implies both pre-existence and immortality.[1] The latter makes immortality a postulate of the practical reason or moral consciousness. In his *Critique of Practical Reason* he says that the moral nature demands of us moral perfection. This, in a being constituted like man, involves endless progression. Such endless progression, of course, necessitates immortality.

[1] "Monadology"; also "Theodicy."

CONCLUSION

THUS, in this elaborate poem, has our author given poetical expression to his thought on some of the profoundest problems that can engage the human mind. He has considered the problem of knowledge and man's capacity to know, and has come to the conclusion that through the Fall of man, and the consequences entailed upon the race thereby, man is suffering from mental impotency — from an impaired mental and moral vision. So that, if man is to know the soul aright, he needs divine aid to supplement his efforts. In the second place, he has considered the problem of the reality of the soul, and has come to the conclusion that the soul is an independent, spiritual agent whose nature is primarily revealed in two fundamental modes of functioning — wit and will. This reality of the soul he has endeavored to vindicate in the face of formidable opposition in the form of Sensationalism and

Materialism, which deny the soul's reality. In
the third place, he has considered the problem
of the mode of the soul's origin — more particularly its origin in connection with the body.
His reflections have led him to reject the doctrines
of Pre-existence and Traducianism, and to adopt
the theory of Creationism — that every soul is
an immediate creation on the part of the Deity
contemporaneously with the body, and is breathed
into the body in its pre-natal state. In the fourth
place, he has considered the problem of the union
of soul and body, and has concluded that the
purpose of this union is, that man might bear the
image of all things — might be a microcosm; also,
that man might utilize and take delight in the
world, as well as glorify the Creator; and, finally,
that man might rule over the animal kingdom.
He has not explained the ultimate nature of the
relation between soul and body, but has likened
this relation unto the union of the morning light
with the atmosphere. In the fifth place, the
poet has considered the question of the soul's
powers and their exercise in the body. In his
psychological analysis he was led to the recognition of the vegetative or quickening power, the
power of sense, and the powers of wit and will,

as constituting the main activities of the soul,
and that these powers are not distinct entities or
agents, but all are modes of the activity of a
distinct unitary agent called mind. He has also
concluded that these powers are mutually dependent, and that the exercise of some is accompanied
by certain physical conditions. In the sixth place,
he has considered the destiny of the mind — the
problem of its immortality, and has come to the
conclusion that it is immortal. In attaining this
conclusion, he has not only considered the arguments in favor of, but also the arguments against,
such belief. And finally, he has concluded that
there are three kinds of life corresponding to the
quickening, sense, and rational powers of the soul.
They are the pre-natal, mortal, and immortal life.
One is hardly surprised that, after such a sustained effort of serious reflection on the problems of a philosophy of mind, and after reaching
such conclusions in regard to the reality, origin,
nature, powers, and destiny of the soul, the poet
finally breaks forth with the acclamation: —

> " O ignorant poor man ! what dost thou beare
>   Lockt vp within the casket of thy brest?
>   What iewels, and what riches hast thou there !
>   What heauenly treasure in so weake a chest !

" Look in thy *soule*, and thou shalt *beauties* find,
    Like those which drownd *Narcissus* in the flood
    Honour and *Pleasure* both are in thy mind,
    And all that in the world is counted *Good*.

" Thinke of her worth, and think that God did meane,
    This worthy mind should worthy things imbrace ;
    Blot not her beauties with thy thoughts vnclean,
    Nor her dishonour with thy passions base ;

" Kill not her *quickning power* with surfettings,
    Mar not her *Sense* with sensualitie ;
    Cast not her serious wit on idle things :
    Make not her free-*will*, slaue to vanitie.

" And when thou think'st of her *eternitie*,
    Thinke not that *Death* against her nature is,
    Thinke it a *birth ;* and when thou goest to die,
    Sing like a swan, as if thou went'st to blisse.

" And if thou, like a child, didst feare before,
    Being in the darke, where thou didst nothing see ;
    Now I haue broght thee *torch-light*, feare no more ;
    Now when thou diest, thou canst not hud-winkt be.

" And thou my *Soule*, which turn'st thy curious eye,
    To view the beames of thine owne forme diuine ;
    Know, that thou canst know nothing perfectly,
    While thou art clouded with this flesh of mine.

" Take heed of *ouer-weening*, and compare
    Thy peacock's feet with thy gay peacock's traine ;
    Study the best, and highest things that are,
    But of thy selfe an humble thought retaine.

" Cast downe thy selfe, and onely striue to raise
  The glory of thy Maker's sacred Name ;
  Vse all thy powers, that Blessed Power to praise,
  Which giues thee power to *bee*, and *vse the same*."

APPENDIX

———

NOSCE TEIPSUM

BY SIR JOHN DAVIES

I. Royal Dedication

TO MY MOST GRACIOVS DREAD SOVERAIGNE

*T*O *that cleere maiestie which in the North*
 Doth, like another Sunne in glory rise;
Which standeth fixt, yet spreads her heauenly
 worth;
Loadstone to hearts, and loadstarre to all eyes.

Like Heau'n in all; like th' Earth in this alone,
 That though great States by her support doe stand,
 Yet she herselfe supported is of none,
 But by the finger of the Almightie's hand:

To the diuinest and the richest minde,
 Both by Art's purchase and by Nature's dowre,
 That euer was from Heau'n to Earth confin'd,
 To shew the vtmost of a creature's power:

To that great Spirit, which doth great kingdomes
 mooue,
 The sacred spring whence right *and* honor
 streames,
 Distilling Vertue, *shedding* Peace *and* Loue,
 In euery place, as Cynthia *sheds her beames:*

I offer up some sparkles of that fire,
  Whereby wee reason, liue, and moue, and be;
  These sparkes by nature euermore aspire,
  Which makes them to so high *an* highnesse *flee.*

Faire Soule, *since to the fairest body knit,*
  You giue such liuely life, such quickning power,
  Such sweet celestiall influences to it,
  As keepes it still in youth's immortall flower :

(As where the sunne is present all the yeere,
  And neuer doth retire his golden ray,
  Needs must the Spring bee euerlasting there,
  And euery season like the month of May.)

O! many, many yeeres may you remaine,
  A happy angell to this happy Land;
  Long, long may you on Earth our empresse raigne,
  Ere you in Heauen a glorious angell stand.

Stay long (sweet spirit) ere thou to Heauen depart,
  Which mak'st each place a heauen wherein thou art.

Her Maiestie's least and vnworthiest Subiect

IOHN DAVIES.

OF HUMANE KNOWLEDGE

WHY did my parents send me to the Schooles,
    That I with knowledge might enrich my
      mind?
  Since the *desire to know* first made men fools,
  And did corrupt the root of all mankind:

For when God's hand had written in the hearts
  Of the first Parents, all the rules of good,
  So that their skill infusde did passe all arts
  That euer were, before, or since the Flood;

And when their reason's eye was sharpe and cleere,
  And (as an eagle can behold the sunne)
  Could haue approcht th' Eternall Light as neere,
  As the intellectuall angels could haue done:

Euen then to them the *Spirit of Lyes* suggests
  That they were blind, because they saw not ill;
  And breathes into their incrupted brests
  A curious *wish*, which did corrupt their *will*.

For that same ill they straight desir'd to know;
  Which ill, being nought but a defect of good,
  In all God's works the Diuell could not show
  While Man their lord in his perfection stood.

So that themselues were first to doe the ill,
 Ere they thereof the knowledge could attaine;
 Like him that knew not poison's power to kill,
 Vntill (by tasting it) himselfe was slaine.

Euen so by tasting of that fruite forbid,
 Where they sought *knowledge*, they did *error*
  find;
 Ill they desir'd to know, and ill they did;
 And to giue *Passion* eyes, made *Reason* blind.

For then their minds did first in Passion see
 Those wretched shapes of *Miserie* and *Woe*,
 Of *Nakednesse*, of *Shame*, of *Pouertie*,
 Which then their owne experience made them
  know.

But then grew *Reason* darke, that *she* no more,
 Could the faire formes of *Good* and *Truth* discern;
 Battes they became, that *eagles* were before:
 And this they got by their *desire to learne*.

But we their wretched of-spring, what doe we?
 Doe not we still taste of the fruit forbid
 Whiles with fond fruitlesse curiositie,
 In bookes prophane we seeke for knowledge
  hid?

What is this *knowledge* but the sky-stolne fire,
   For which the *thiefe* still chain'd in ice doth sit?
   And which the poore rude *Satyre* did admire,
   And needs would kisse but burnt his lips with it.

What is it? but the cloud of emptie raine,
   Which when *Ioue's* guest imbrac't, hee monsters
      got?
   Or the false *payles* which oft being fild with paine,
   Receiv'd the water, but retain'd it not!

Shortly, what is it but the firie coach
   Which the *Youth* sought, and sought his death
      withal?
   Or the *boye's* wings, which when he did approch
   The *sunne's* hot beames, did melt and let him fall?

And yet alas, when all our lamps are burnd,
   Our bodyes wasted, and our spirits spent;
   When we haue all the learnèd *Volumes* turn'd,
   Which yeeld mens wits both help and ornament:

What can we know? or what can we discerne?
   When *Error* chokes the windowes of the minde,
   The diuers formes of things, how can we learne,
   That haue been euer from our birth-day blind?

15

When *Reasone's* lampe, which (like the *sunne* in
    skie)
    Throughout *Man's* little world her beames did
        spread;
    Is now become a sparkle, which doth lie
    Vnder the ashes, halfe extinct, and dead:

How can we hope, that through the eye and eare,
    This dying sparkle, in this cloudy place,
    Can recollect these beames of knowledge cleere,
    Which were infus'd in the first minds by grace?

So might the heire whose father hath in play
    Wasted a thousand pound of ancient rent;
    By painefull earning of a groate a day,
    Hope to restore the patrimony spent.

The wits that diu'd most deepe and soar'd most hie
    Seeking Man's pow'rs, haue found his weaknesse
        such:
    " Skill comes so slow, and life so fast doth flie,
    " We learne so little and forget so much.

For this the wisest of all morall men
    Said, ' *He knew nought, but that he nought did
        know* ' ;
    And the great mocking-Master mockt not then,
    When he said, ' *Truth was buried deepe below.*'

For how may we to others' things attaine,
    When none of vs his owne soule vnderstands?
    For which the Diuell mockes our curious braine,
    When, '*Know thy selfe*' his oracle commands.

For why should wee the busie Soule beleeue,
    When boldly she concludes of that and this;
    When of her selfe she can no iudgement giue,
    Nor how, nor whence, nor where, nor what she is?

All things without, which round about we see,
    We seeke to knowe, and how therewith to doe;
    But that whereby we *reason, liue and be*,
    Within our selues, we strangers are thereto.

We seeke to know the mouing of each spheare,
    And the strange cause of th' ebs and flouds of
        Nile ;
    But of that clocke within our breasts we beare,
    The subtill motions we forget the while.

We that acquaint our selues with euery *Zoane*
    And passe both *Tropikes* and behold the *Poles*,
    When we come home, are to our selues vn-
        known,
    And vnacquainted still with our owne *Soules.*

We study *Speech* but others we perswade;
    We *leech-craft* learne, but others cure with it;
    We interpret *lawes*, which other men haue made,
    But reade not those which in our hearts are writ.

Is it because the minde is like the eye,
    Through which it gathers knowledge by de-
        grees —
    Whose rayes reflect not, but spread outwardly:
    Not seeing it selfe when other things it sees?

No, doubtlesse; for the mind can backward cast
    Vpon her selfe, her vnderstanding light;
    But she is so corrupt, and so defac't,
    As her owne image doth her selfe affright.

As in the fable of the Lady faire,
    Which for her lust was turnd into a cow;
    When thirstie to a streame she did repaire,
    And saw her selfe transform'd she wist not how:

At first she startles, then she stands amaz'd,
    At last with terror she from thence doth flye;
    And loathes the watry glasse wherein she gaz'd,
    And shunnes it still, though she for thirst doe
        die:

Euen so *Man's Soule* which did God's image beare,
  And was at first faire, good, and spotlesse pure;
  Since with her *sinnes* her beauties blotted were,
  Doth of all sights her owne sight least endure:

For euen at first reflection she espies,
  Such strange *chimeraes*, and such monsters there;
  Such toyes, such *antikes*, and such vanities,
  As she retires, and shrinkes for shame and feare.

And as the man loues least at home to bee,
  That hath a sluttish house haunted with *sprites;*
  So she impatient her owne faults to see,
  Turnes from her selfe and in strange things delites.

For this few *know themselues:* for merchants broke
  View their estate with discontent and paine;
  And *seas* are troubled, when they doe reuoke
  Their flowing waues into themselues againe.

And while the face of outward things we find,
  Pleasing and faire, agreeable and sweet;
  These things transport, and carry out the mind,
  That with her selfe her selfe can neuer meet.

Yet if *Affliction* once her warres begin,
  And threat the feebler *Sense* with sword and fire;
  The *Minde* contracts her selfe and shrinketh in,
  And to her selfe she gladly doth retire:

As *Spiders* toucht, seek their webs inmost part;
　As *bees* in stormes vnto their hiues returne;
　As bloud in danger gathers to the heart;
　As men seek towns, when foes the country burn.

If ought can teach vs ought, *Afflictions* lookes,
　(Making vs looke into our selues so neere,)
　Teach vs to *know our selues* beyond all bookes,
　Or all the learned Schooles that euer were.

This *mistresse* lately pluckt me by the eare,
　And many a golden lesson hath me taught;
　Hath made my *Senses* quicke, and Reason cleare,
　Reform'd my Will and rectifide my Thought.

So doe the *winds* and *thunders* cleanse the ayre;
　So working lees settle and purge the wine;
　So lop't and prunèd trees doe flourish faire;
　So doth the fire the drossie gold refine.

Neither *Minerua* nor the learnèd Muse,
　Nor rules of *Art*, nor *precepts* of the wise;
　Could in my braine those beames of skill infuse,
　As but the glance of this *Dame's* angry eyes.

She within *lists* my ranging minde hath brought,
　That now beyond my selfe I list not goe;
　My selfe am *center* of my circling thought,
　Onely *my selfe* I studie, learne, and know.

I know my bodie's of so fraile a kind,
    As force without, feauers within can kill;
    I know the heauenly nature of my minde,
    But 'tis corrupted both in wit and will:

I know my *Soule* hath power to know all things,
    Yet is she blinde and ignorant in all;
    I know I am one of Nature's little kings,
    Yet to the least and vilest things am thrall.

I know my life's a paine and but a span,
    I know my *Sense* is mockt with euery thing:
    And to conclude, I know my selfe a MAN,
    Which is a *proud*, and yet a *wretched* thing.

OF THE SOULE OF MAN AND THE IMMORTALITE THEREOF

THE lights of heau'n (which are the World's
    fair eies)
Looke downe into the World, the World to see;
And as they turne, or wander in the skies,
Suruey all things that on this *Center* bee.

And yet the *lights* which in my *towre* do shine,
    Mine *eyes* which view all obiects, nigh and farre;
Looke not into this little world of mine,
    Nor see my face, wherein they fixèd are.

Since *Nature* failes vs in no needfull thing,
    Why want I meanes my inward selfe to see?
Which sight the knowledg of my self might bring,
    Which to true wisdome is the first degree.

That *Power* which gaue me eyes the World to view,
    To see my selfe infus'd an *inward light;*
Whereby my *Soule,* as by a mirror true,
    Of her owne forme may take a perfect sight,

But as the sharpest *eye* discerneth nought,
 Except the *sunne*-beames in the ayre doe shine;
 So the best *Soule* with her reflecting thought,
 Sees not her selfe without some light diuine.

O Light which mak'st the light, which makes the
   day!
 Which setst the eye without, and mind within;
 'Lighten my spirit with one cleare heauenly ray,
 Which now to view it selfe doth first begin.

For her true forme how can my sparke discerne?
 Which dimme by *nature*, *Art* did neuer cleare;
 When the great wits, of whom all skill we learn,
 Are ignorant both *what* shee is, and *where*.

One thinks the *Soule* is *aire;* another, *fire;*
 Another *blood*, diffus'd about the heart;
 Another saith, the *elements* conspire,
 And to her *essence* each doth giue a part.

Musicians thinke our *Soules* are *harmonies*,
 Phisicians hold that they *complexions* bee;
 Epicures make them swarmes of *atomies*,
 Which doe by chance into our bodies flee.

Some thinke one generall *Soule* fils euery braine,
 As the bright *sunne* sheds light in euery starre;
 And others thinke the name of *Soule* is vaine,
 And that we onely *well-mixt* bodies are.

In judgement of her *substance* thus they vary ;
    And thus they vary in iudgement of her *seat ;*
    For some her chaire vp to the braine doe
        carry,
    Some thrust it downe into the *stomackes* heat.

Some place it in the root of life, the *heart ;*
    Some in the *liuer*, fountaine of the veines;
    Some say, *Shee is all in all, and all in part :*
    Some say, She is not containd but all containes.

Thus these great clerks their little wisdome show,
    While with their doctrines they at *hazard* play,
    Tossing their light opinions to and fro,
    To mocke the *lewd*, as learn'd in this as they.

For no craz'd braine could euer yet propound,
    Touching the *Soule*, so vaine and fond a thought,
    But some among these masters haue been
        found,
    Which in their *Schooles* the self-same thing haue
        taught.

God onely wise, to punish pride of wit,
    Among men's wits hath this confusion wrought,
    As the proud *towre* whose points the clouds did
        hit,
    By tongues' confusion was to ruine brought.

But *Thou* which didst *Man's soule* of nothing
    make,
  And when to nothing it was fallen agen,
  "To make it new, the forme of man didst take,
  "And *God* with *God*, becam'st a *Man* with
    men.

Thou, that hast fashioned twice this *Soule* of ours,
  So that she is by double title Thine :
  Thou onely knowest her nature and her pow'rs,
  Her subtill forme Thou onely canst define.

To iudge her selfe she must her selfe transcend,
  As greater circles comprehend the lesse ;
  But she wants power, her owne powers to ex-
    tend,
  As fettered men can not their strength expresse.

But Thou bright Morning Star, Thou rising *Sunne*,
  Which in these later times hast brought to
    light
  Those mysteries, that since the world begun,
  Lay hid in darknesse, and eternall night:

Thou (*like the sunne*) dost with indifferent ray,
  Into the *palace* and the *cottage* shine,
  And shew'st the *soule* both to the clerke and lay,
  By the cleare *lampe* of Thy *Oracle* diuine.

This Lampe through all the regions of my braine,
  Where my *soule* sits, doth spread such beames
      of grace,
  As now, me thinks, I do distinguish plain,
  Each subtill line of her immortall face.

WHAT THE SOULE IS

The soule a substance, and a *spirit* is,
  Which *God* Himselfe doth in the body make ;
  Which makes the *Man :* for euery man from
      this,
  The *nature* of a *Man*, and *name* doth take.

And though this spirit be to the body knit,
  As an apt meane her powers to exercise ;
  Which are *life*, *motion*, *sense*, and *will*, and *wit*,
  Yet she *suruiues*, although the body *dies*.

THAT THE SOULE IS A THING SUBSISTING BY IT SELFE WITHOUT THE BODY

S*HE is a substance*, and a reall thing,
    Which hath it selfe an actuall working might ;
  Which neither from the Senses' power doth
      spring,
  Nor from the bodie's humors, tempred right.

She is a *vine*, which doth no propping need,
  To make her spread her selfe or spring vpright;
She is a *starre*, whose beames doe not proceed
  From any *sunne*, but from a *natiue* light.

For when she sorts things *present* with things *past*,
  And thereby things to *come* doth oft foresee;
When she doth *doubt* at first, and *chuse* at last,
  These acts her owne, without her body bee.

When of the deaw, which the *eye* and *eare* doe take
  From flowers abroad, and bring into the braine,
She doth within both waxe and hony make:
  This worke is her's, this is her proper paine.

When she from sundry acts, one skill doth draw,
  Gathering from diuers fights one art of warre,
From many cases like, one rule of Law;
  These her collections, not the *Senses* are.

When in th' effects she doth the causes know,
  And seeing the stream, thinks wher the spring
    doth rise;
  And seeing the branch, conceiues the root below;
  These things she views without the bodie's eyes.

When she, without a *Pegasus*, doth flie
  Swifter then lightning's fire from *East* to *West*,
About the *Center* and aboue the *skie*,
  She trauels then, although the body rest.

When all her works she formeth first within,
  Proportions them, and sees their perfect end,
  Ere she in act does anie part begin;
  What instruments doth then the body lend?

When without hands she doth thus *castles* build,
  Sees without eyes, and without feet doth runne;
  When she digests the world, yet is not fil'd:
  By her owne power these miracles are done.

When she defines, argues, diuides, compounds,
  Considers *vertue, vice,* and *generall things,*
  And marrying diuers principles and grounds,
  Out of their match a true conclusion brings.

These actions in her closet all alone,
  (Retir'd within her selfe) she doth fulfill;
  Vse of her bodie's organs she hath none,
  When she doth vse the powers of Wit and Will.

Yet in the bodie's prison so she lies,
  As through the bodie's windowes she must looke,
  Her diuers powers of *sense* to exercise,
  By gath'ring notes out of the *World's* great book.

Nor can her selfe discourse or iudge of ought,
  But what the *Sense* collects and home doth bring;
  And yet the power of her discoursing thought,
  From these collections, is a diuers thing.

For though our eyes can nought but colours see,
   Yet colours giue them not their powre of sight;
So, though these fruits of *Sense* her obiects bee,
   Yet she discernes them by her proper light.

The workman on his stuffe his skill doth show,
   And yet the stuffe giues not the man his skill;
Kings their affaires do by their seruants know,
   But order them by their owne royall will.

So, though this cunning mistresse and this queene,
   Doth, as her instrument, the *Senses* vse,
To know all things that are *felt*, *heard*, or *seene*,
   Yet she her selfe doth onely *iudge* and *chuse:*

Euen as our great wise *Empresse* that now raignes
   By *soueraigne* title ouer sundry Lands;
Borrowes in meane affaires her *subiects* paines,
   Sees by their eyes, and writeth by their hands;

But things of waight and consequence indeed,
   Her selfe doth in her chamber them debate;
Where all her Counsellers she doth exceed
   As farre in iudgement, as she doth in State.

Or as the man whom she doth now aduance,
   Vpon her gracious *mercy-seat* to sit;
Doth common things, of course and circumstance,
   To the reports of common men commit:

But when the cause it selfe must be decreed,
 Himselfe in person, in his proper Court,
 To graue and solemne hearing doth proceed,
 Of euery proofe and euery by-report.

Then, like God's angell he pronounceth right,
 And milke and hony from his tongue doth flow;
 Happie are they that still are in his sight,
 To reape the wisedome which his lips doe sow.

Right so the *Soule*, which is a lady free,
 And doth the iustice of her *State* maintaine;
 Because the senses ready seruants be,
 Attending nigh about her Court, the braine:

By them the formes of outward things she learnes,
 For they returne into the fantasie,
 What euer each of them abroad discernes,
 And there inrole it for the Minde to see.

But when she sits to iudge the good and ill,
 And to discerne betwixt the false and true;
 She is not guided by the *Senses'* skill,
 But doth each thing in her owne mirrour view.

Then she the *Senses* checks, which oft do erre,
 And euen against their false reports decrees;
 And oft she doth condemne what they preferre,
 For with a power aboue the *Sense*, she sees.

Therefore no *Sense* the precious ioyes conceiues,
 Which in her priuate contemplations bee;
 For then the rauish't spirit the *Senses* leaues,
 Hath her owne powers, and proper actions free.

Her harmonies are sweet, and full of skill,
 When on the Bodie's instrument she playes;
 But the proportions of the *wit* and *will*,
 Those sweete accords, are euen the angel's layes.

These tunes of *Reason* are *Amphion's* lyre,
 Wherewith he did the *Thebane* citie found;
 These are the notes wherewith the heauenly *quire*,
 The praise of Him which made the heauen doth
 sound.

Then her *selfe-being nature* shines in this,
 That she performes her noblest works alone;
 "The *worke*, the touch-stone of the *nature* is,
 " And by their operations, things are knowne.

THAT THE SOULE IS MORE THEN A PERFECTION OR REFLECTION OF THE SENSE

A RE *they not sencelesse* then, that thinke the
 Soule
 Nought but a fine perfection of the *Sense;*
 Or of the formes which *fancie* doth enroule,
 A *quicke resulting*, and a *consequence?*

16

What is it then that doth the *Sense* accuse,
  Both of *false judgements*, and *fond appetites ?*
  What makes vs do what *Sense* doth most refuse?
  Which oft in torment of the *Sense* delights?

Sense thinkes the *planets, spheares* not much
      asunder;
  What tels vs then their distance is so farre?
  Sense thinks the lightning borne before the
      thunder;
  What tels vs then they both together are?

When men seem crows far off vpon a towre,
  Sense saith, th' are crows; what makes vs think
      them men?
  When we in *agues*, thinke all sweete things sowre,
  What makes vs know our tongue's false iudge-
      ment then?

What power was that, whereby *Medea* saw,
  And well approu'd, and prais'd the better course,
  When her rebellious *Sense* did so withdraw
  Her feeble powers, as she pursu'd the worse?

Did *Sense* perswade *Vlisses* not to heare
  The mermaid's songs, which so his men did
      please;
  As they were all perswaded, through the eare
  To quit the ship, and leape into the *seas ?*

Could any power of *Sense* the *Romane* moue,
　To burn his own right hand with courage stout?
Could *Sense* make *Marius* sit vnbound, and
　　proue
The cruell lancing of the knotty gout?

Doubtlesse in *Man* there is a *nature* found,
　Beside the *Senses*, and aboue them farre;
　"Though most men being in sensuall pleasures
　　drownd,
　"It seemes their *Soules* but in their *Senses* are.

If we had nought but *Sense*, then onely they
　Should haue sound minds, which haue their
　　Senses sound;
　But *Wisdome* growes, when *Senses* doe decay,
And *Folly* most in quickest *Sense* is found.

If we had nought but *Sense*, each liuing wight,
　Which we call *brute*, would be more sharp then
　　we;
　As hauing *Sense's apprehensiue might*,
In a more cleere, and excellent degree.

But they doe want that *quicke discoursing power*,
　Which doth in vs the erring *Sense* correct;
Therefore the *bee* did sucke the painted flower,
And *birds*, of grapes, the cunning shadow, peckt.

Sense outsides knows; the Soule throgh al things
     sees;
  Sense, circumstance; she, doth the *substance*
     view;
  Sense sees the barke, but she, the life of trees;
  Sense heares the sounds, but she, the concords
     true.

But why doe I the *Soule* and *Sense* diuide?
  When *Sense* is but a power, which she extends;
  Which being in diuers parts diuersifide,
  The diuers formes of obiects apprehends?

This power spreds outward, but the root doth grow
  In th' inward *Soule*, which onely doth perceiue;
  For th' *eyes* and *eares* no more their obiects
     know,
  Then glasses know what faces they receiue.

For if we chance to fixe our thoughts elsewhere,
  Although our eyes be ope, we cannot see;
  And if one power did not both see and heare,
  Our sights and sounds would alwayes double be.

Then is the *Soule* a nature, which containes
  The powre of *Sense*, within a greater power
  Which doth imploy and vse the *Senses* paines,
  But sits and rules within her priuate bower.

THAT THE SOULE IS MORE THEN THE TEMPERATURE OF THE HUMORS OF THE BODY

IF shee doth then the subtill *Sense* excell,
  How gross are they that drown her in the
    blood!
  Or in the bodie's humors tempred well,
  As if in them such high perfection stood?

As if most skill in that *Musician* were,
  Which had the best, and best tun'd instrument;
  As if the pensill neate and colours cleare,
  Had power to make the Painter excellent.

Why doth not beautie then refine the wit?
  And good complexion rectifie the will?
  Why doth not health bring wisdom still with it?
  Why doth not sicknesse make men bruitish still?

Who can in *memory*, or *wit*, or *will*,
  Or *ayre*, or *fire*, or *earth*, or *water* finde?
  What alchymist can draw, with all his skil,
  The *quintessence* of these, out of the mind?

If th' *elements* which haue nor *life*, nor *sense*,
  Can breed in vs so great a powre as this;
  Why giue they not themselues like excellence,
  Or other things wherein their mixture is?

If she were but the Bodie's qualitie
   Then would she be with it *sicke, maim'd* and
      blind;
   But we perceiue where these priuations be
   A *healthy, perfect,* and *sharpe-sighted* mind.

If she the bodie's nature did pertake,
   Her strength would with the bodie's strength
      decay;
   But when the bodie's strongest sinewes slake,
   Then is the *Soule* most actiue, quicke and
      gay.

If she were but the bodie's accident,
   And her sole *being* did in it subsist;
   As *white in snow;* she might her selfe absent,
   And in the bodie's substance not be mist.

But *it* on *her,* not *shee* on *it* depends;
   For *shee* the body doth sustaine and cherish;
   Such secret powers of life to it she lends,
   That when they faile, then doth the body
      perish.

Since then the *Soule works by her selfe alone,*
   Springs not from Sense, nor humors, well agreeing;
   Her nature is peculiar, and her owne:
   She is a *substance,* and a *perfect being.*

THAT THE SOULE IS A SPIRIT

B UT though this substance be the root of *Sense*,
   Sense knowes her not, which doth but *bodies*
     know;
 Shee is a spirit, and heauenly influence,
 Which from the fountaine of God's Spirit doth
   flow.

Shee is a Spirit, yet not like *ayre*, or *winde*,
   Nor like the *spirits* about the *heart* or *braine;*
   Nor like those spirits which alchymists do find,
   When they in euery thing seeke gold in *vaine.*

For shee all *natures* vnder heauen doth passe;
   Being like those spirits, which God's bright face
     do see;
   Or like *Himselfe*, Whose *image* once she was,
   Though now (alas!) she scarce His *shadow* bee.

Yet of the *formes*, she holds the first degree,
   That are to grosse materiall bodies knit;
   Yet shee her selfe is *bodilesse* and free;
   And though confin'd, is almost infinite.

That it cannot be a Body

Were she a *body* how could she remaine
  Within this body, which is lesse then she?
  Or how could she the world's great shape contain,
  And in our narrow brests containèd bee?

All *bodies* are confin'd within some place,
  But *she* all place within her selfe confines;
  All *bodies* haue their measure, and their space,
  But who can draw the *Soule's* dimensiue lines?

No *body* can at once two formes admit,
  Except the one the other doe deface;
  But in the *soule* ten thousand formes do sit,
  And none intrudes into her neighbour's place.

All *bodies* are with other bodies fild,
  But she receiues both heauen and earth together;
  Nor are their formes by rash incounter spild,
  For there they stand, and neither toucheth either.

Nor can her wide imbracements fillèd bee;
  For they that most, and greatest things embrace,
  Inlarge thereby their minds' capacitie,
  As streames inlarg'd, inlarge the channel's space.

All things receiu'd, doe such proportion take,
  As those things haue, wherein they are receiu'd:
  So little glasses little faces make,
  And narrow webs on narrow frames be weau'd;

Then what vast body must we make the *mind*
  Wherin are men, beasts, trees, towns, seas, and
      lands;
  And yet each thing a proper place doth find,
  And each thing in the true proportion stands?

Doubtlesse this could not bee, but that she turnes
  Bodies to spirits, by *sublimation* strange;
  As fire conuerts to fire the things it burnes
  As we our meats into our nature change.

From their grosse *matter* she abstracts the *formes*,
  And drawes a kind of *quintessence* from things;
  Which to her proper nature she transformes,
  To bear them light on her celestiall wings:

This doth she, when, from things *particular*,
  She doth abstract the *universall kinds;*
  Which bodilesse and immateriall are,
  And can be lodg'd but onely in our minds:

And thus from diuers *accidents* and *acts*,
  Which doe within her obseruation fall,
  She goddesses, and powers diuine, abstracts:
  As *Nature, Fortune*, and the *Vertues* all.

Againe, how can she seuerall *bodies* know,
    If in her selfe a *bodie's* forme she beare?
    How can a mirror sundry faces show,
    If from all shapes and formes it be not cleare?

Nor could we by our eyes all colours learne,
    Except our eyes were of all colours voide;
    Nor sundry tastes can any tongue discerne,
    Which is with grosse and bitter humors cloide.

Nor may a man of *passions* iudge aright,
    Except his minde bee from all passions free;
    Nor can a *Iudge* his office well acquite,
    If he possest of either partie bee.

If lastly, this quicke power a body were,
    Were it as swift as is the *winde* or *fire*;
    (Whose atomies doe th' one down side-waies
        beare,
    And make the other in *pyramids* aspire:)

Her nimble body yet in time must moue,
    And not in instants through all places slide;
    But she is nigh, and farre, beneath, aboue,
    In point of time, which thought cannot deuide:

She is sent as soone to *China* as to *Spaine*,
    And thence returnes, as soone as shee is sent;
    She measures with one time, and with one paine,
    An ell of silke, and heauen's wide spreading tent.

As then the *Soule* a substance hath alone,
　Besides the Body in which she is confin'd;
　So hath she not a *body* of her owne,
　But is a *spirit*, and *immateriall minde*.

THAT THE SOULE IS CREATED IMMEDIATELY BY GOD

Since body and soule haue such diuersities,
　Well might we muse, how first their match began;
　But that we learne, that He that spread the skies,
　And fixt the Earth, first form'd the *soule* in man.

This true *Prometheus* first made Man of earth,
　And shed in him a beame of heauenly fire;
　Now in their mother's wombs before their birth,
　Doth in all sonnes of men their *soules* inspire.

And as *Minerua* is in fables said,
　From *Ioue*, without a mother to proceed;
　So our true *Ioue*, without a mother's ay'd,
　Doth daily millions of *Mineruas* breed.

ERRONIOUS OPINIONS OF THE CREATION OF SOULES

THEN neither from eternitie before,
    Nor from the time when *Time's* first point
        begun;
  Made He all *soules·* which now he keepes in
    store,
  Some in the moone, and others in the sunne:

Nor in a *secret cloyster* doth Hee keepe
  These virgin-spirits, vntill their marriage-day;
  Nor locks them vp in chambers, where they
    sleep,
  Till they awake, within these beds of clay.

Nor did He first a certaine number make,
  Infusing part in *beasts*, and part in *men*,
  And, as vnwilling further paines to take,
  Would make no more then those He framèd then.

So that the widow *Soule* her *body* dying,
  Vnto the next-borne *body* married was;
  And so by often changing and supplying,
  Mens' *soules* to beasts, and beasts to men did
    passe.

(These thoughts are fond; for since the bodies
    borne
  Be more in number farre then those that dye;
  Thousands must be abortiue, and forlorne,
  Ere others' deaths to them their *soules* supply.)

But as *God's handmaid*, *Nature*, doth create
  Bodies in time distinct, and order due;
  So God giues *soules* the like successiue date,
  Which *Him selfe* makes, in bodies formèd new:

Which *Him selfe* makes, of no materiall thing;
  For vnto angels He no power hath giuen,
  Either to forme the shape, or stuffe to bring
  From *ayre* or *fire*, or *substance of the heauen*.

Nor He in this doth *Nature's* seruice vse;
  For though from bodies, she can bodies bring,
  Yet could she neuer soules from Soules *traduce*,
  As fire from fire, or light from light doth spring.

OBJECTION: — THAT THE SOULE IS EXTRADUCE

A LAS! that some, that were great lights of old,
    And in their hands the *lampe* of God did
    beare;
  Some reuerend Fathers did this error hold,
  Hauing their eyes dim'd with religious feare!

For when (say they) by Rule of Faith we find,
  That euery *soule* vnto her *body* knit,
  Brings from the mother's wombe, the *sinne of kind*,
  The roote of all the ills she doth commit

How can we say that God the *Soule* doth make,
  But we must make Him author of her sinne?
  Then from man's soule she doth beginning take,
  Since in man's soule corruption did begin.

For if God make her, first He makes her ill,
  (Which God forbid our thoghts should yeeld vnto!)
  Or makes the body her faire forme to spill,
  Which, of it selfe it had no power to doe.

Not *Adam's body* but his *soule* did sinne
  And so her selfe vnto corruption brought;
  But the poore *soule* corrupted is within,
  Ere shee had sinn'd, either in act, or thought:

And yet we see in her such powres diuine,
  As we could gladly thinke, *from God she came ;*
  Faine would we make Him Author of the wine,
  If for the dregs we could some other blame.

THE ANSWERE TO THE OBIECTION

*T*HUS *these* good men with holy zeale were
   blind,
When on the other part the truth did shine;
Whereof we doe cleare demonstrations find,
By light of *Nature,* and by light *Diuine.*

None are so grosse as to contend for this,
   That soules from bodies may traducèd bee;
   Betweene whose natures no proportion is,
   When roote and branch in nature still agree.

But many subtill wits haue iustifi'd,
   That *soules* from *soules* spiritually may spring;
   Which (if the nature of the *soule* be tri'd)
   Will euen in Nature proue as grosse a thing.

REASONS DRAWNE FROM NATURE

*F*OR all things made, are either made of nought,
   Or made of stuffe that ready made doth
      stand;
Of nought no creature euer formèd ought,
For that is proper to th' Almightie's hand.

If then the *soule* another *soule* doe make,
　Because her power is kept within a bound,
　Shee must some former stuffe or *matter* take;
　But in the soule there is no *matter* found.

Then if her heauenly Forme doe not agree
　With any *matter* which the world containes;
　Then she of nothing must created bee,
　And to *create*, to God alone pertaines.

Againe, if *soules* doe other *soules* beget,
　'T is by themselues, or by the bodie's power;
　If by themselues, what doth their working let,
　But they might *soules* engender euery houre?

If by the body, how can *wit* and *will*
　Ioyne with the body onely in this act?
　Sith when they doe their other works fulfill,
　They from the body doe themselues *abstract?*

Againe, if *soules* of *soules* begotten were,
　Into each other they should change and moue;
　And *change* and *motion still corruption* beare;
　How shall we then the *soule* immortall proue?

If lastly, *soules* doe generation vse,
　Then should they spread incorruptible seed;
　What then becomes of that which they doe lose,
　When th' acts of generation doe not speed?

And though the *soule* could cast spirituall seed,
  Yet *would* she not, because she *neuer dies;*
  For mortall things desire their *like* to breed,
  That so they may their kind immortalize.

Therefore the angels, sonnes of God are nam'd,
  And marry not, nor are in marriage giuen;
  Their spirits and ours are of one *substance* fram'd,
  And haue one Father, euen the *Lord of heauen:*

Who would at first, that in each other thing,
  The *earth* and *water* liuing *soules* should breed;
  But that *man's soule* whom He would make their king,
  Should from Himselfe immediatly proceed.

And when He took the *woman* from *man's* side,
  Doubtlesse Himselfe inspir'd her *soule* alone;
  For 't is not said, He did *man's soule* diuide,
  But took *flesh of his flesh, bone of his bone.*

Lastly, God being made Man for man's owne sake,
  And being like Man in all, except in sin,
  His body from the *virgin's* wombe did take;
  But all agree, *God form'd His soule within.*

Then is the *soule* from God; so *Pagans* say,
  Which saw by *Nature's* light her heauenly kind;
  Naming her *kin to God, and God's bright ray,*
  A citizen of Heauen to Earth confined.

17

But now, I feele, they plucke me by the eare
  Whom my young *Muse* so boldly termèd blind;
  And craue more heauenly light, that cloud to clear,
  Which makes them think God doth not make
    the mind.

Reasons drawne from Diuinity

GOD doubtlesse makes her, and doth make her
    good,
  And graffes her in the body, there to spring;
  Which, though it be corrupted, flesh and blood
  Can no way to the *Soule* corruption bring:

And yet this *Soule* (made good by God at first,
  And not corrupted by the bodie's ill)
  Euen in the wombe is sinfull, and accurst,
  Ere shee can *iudge* by *wit* or *chuse* by *will*.

Yet is not God the Author of her sinne
  Though Author of her *being*, and *being there;*
  And if we dare to iudge our *Iudge* herein,
  He can condemne vs, and Himselfe can cleare.

First, God from infinite eternitie
  Decreed, what *hath beene, is,* or *shall bee* done;
  And was resolu'd, that euery man should bee,
  And in his turne, his race of life should run:

And so did purpose all the *soules* to make,
   That euer *haue beene* made, or *euer shall;*
   And that their *being* they should onely take
   In humane bodies, or not *bee* at all.

Was it then fit that such a weake euent
   (*W[e]aknesse it selfe,* — the sinne and fall of
      Man)
   His counsel's execution should preuent,
   Decreed and fixt before the World began?

Or that one *penall law* by *Adam* broke,
   Should make God breake His owne *eternall
      Law;*
   The setled order of the World reuoke,
   And change all forms of things, which He fore-
      saw?

Could *Eue's* weake hand, extended to the tree,
   In sunder rend that *adamantine chaine,*
   Whose golden links, *effects* and causes be,
   And which to God's owne chair doth fixt re-
      maine.

O could we see, how cause from cause doth spring!
   How mutually they linkt and folded are!
   And heare how oft one disagreeing string
   The harmony doth rather make then marre?

And view at once, how *death* by *sinne* is brought,
   And how from *death*, a better *life* doth rise,
   How this God's *iustice*, and His *mercy* tought :
   We this decree would praise, as right and wise.

But we that measure times by first and last,
   The sight of things successiuely, doe take ;
   When God on all at once His view doth cast,
   And of all times doth but one *instant* make.

All in *Himselfe* as in a *glasse* Hee sees,
   For *from Him, by Him, through Him, all things bee:*
   His sight is not discoursiue, by degrees,
   But seeing the whole, each single part doth see.

He lookes on *Adam*, as a *root*, or *well*,
   And on his heires, as *branches*, and as *streames ;*
   He sees *all* men as *one* Man, though they dwell
   In sundry cities, and in sundry realmes :

And as the *roote* and *branch* are but one *tree*,
   And *well* and *streame* doe but one *riuer* make ;
   So, if the *root* and *well* corrupted bee,
   The *streame* and *branch* the same corruption take :

So, when the root and fountaine of Mankind
   Did draw corruption, and God's curse, by sin ;
   This was a charge that all his heires did bind,
   And all his offspring grew corrupt therein.

And· as when the hand doth strike, the Man offends,
   (For *part from whole, Law seuers not in this*)
   So *Adam's* sinne to the whole kind extends;
   For all their natures are but part of his.

Therefore this *sinne of kind*, not personall,
   But reall and hereditary was;
   The guilt whereof, and punishment to all,
   By course of Nature, and of Law doth passe.

For as that easie Law was giuen to all,
   To ancestor and heire, to first and last;
   So was the first transgression generall,
   And all did plucke the fruit and all did tast.

Of this we find some foot-steps in our Law,
   Which doth her root from God and Nature take;
   Ten thousand men she doth together draw,
   And of them all, one Corporation make:

Yet these, and their successors, are but one,
   And if they gaine or lose their liberties;
   They harme, or profit not themselues alone,
   But such as in succeeding times shall rise.

And so the ancestor, and all his heires,
   Though they in number passe the stars of heauen
   Are still but one; his forfeitures are theirs,
   And vnto them are his aduancements giuen:

His ciuill acts doe binde and bar them all;
   And as from *Adam*, all corruption take,
   So, if the father's crime be *capitall*
   In all the *bloud*, Law doth *corruption* make.

Is it then iust with vs, to dis-inherit
   The vnborn nephewes for the father's fault?
   And to aduance againe for one man's merit,
   A thousand heires, that have deservèd nought?

And is not God's decree as iust as ours,
   If He, for *Adam's* sinne, his sonnes depriue,
   Of all those natiue vertues, and those powers,
   Which He to him, and to his race did giue?

For what is this contagious sinne of kinde
   But a priuation of that grace within?
   And of that great rich dowry of the minde
   Which all had had, but for the first man's sin?

If then a man, on light conditions gaine
   A great estate, to him and his, for euer;
   If wilfully he forfeit it againe
   Who doth bemone his heire or blame the giuer?

So, though God make the *Soule* good, rich and faire,
   Yet when her forme is to the body knit,
   Which makes the Man, which man is *Adam's*
      heire
   Iustly forth-with He takes His grace from it:

And then the soule being first from nothing
    brought,
  When God's grace failes her, doth to nothing fall ;
  And this *declining pronenesse vnto nought,*
  Is euen that sinne that we are borne withall.

Yet not alone the first good qualities,
  Which in the first *soule* were, depriuèd are ;
  But in their place the contrary doe rise,
  And reall spots of sinne her beauty marre.

Nor is it strange, that Adam's ill desart
  Should be transferd vnto his guilty Race ;
  When Christ His grace and iustice doth impart
  To men vniust, and such as haue no grace.

Lastly, the *Soule* were better so to bee
  Borne slaue to sinne, then not to be at all ;
  Since (if she do belieue) One sets her free,
  That makes her mount the higher for her fall.

Yet this the curious wits will not content ;
  They yet will know (sith God foresaw this ill)
  Why His high Prouidence did not preuent
  The declination of the first man's will.

If by His Word He had the current staid
  Of *Adam's* will, which was by nature free ;
  It had bene one, as if His Word had said,
  I will henceforth that *Man no man shall bee.*

For what is Man without a moouing mind,
  Which hath a iudging *wit*, and chusing *will?*
  Now, if God's power should her election bind,
  Her motions then would cease and stand all still.

And why did God in man this *soule* infuse,
  But that he should his Maker *know* and *loue?*
  Now, if *loue* be compeld and cannot chuse,
  How can it gratefull or thankeworthy proue?

Loue must free-hearted be, and voluntary,
  And not enchanted, or by Fate constraind;
  Nor like that loue, which did *Ulisses* carry,
  To *Circe's* ile, with mighty charmes enchaind.

Besides, were we vnchangeable in *will*,
  And of a *wit* that nothing could mis-deeme;
  Equall to God, Whose wisedome shineth still,
  And neuer erres, we might our selues esteeme.

So that if Man would be vnuariable,
  He must be God, or like a rock or tree;
  For euen the perfect Angels were not stable,
  But had a fall more desperate then wee.

Then let vs praise that Power, which makes vs be
  Men as we are, and rest contented so;
  And knowing Man's fall was curiositie,
  Admire God's counsels, which we cannot know.

And let vs know that God the Maker is
    Of all the *Soules*, in all the men that be:
    Yet their corruption is no fault of His,
    But the first man's that broke God's first decree.

WHY THE SOULE IS UNITED TO THE BODY

THIS *substance*, and this *spirit of God's owne
    making*,
    Is in the body plact, and planted heere;
    " That both of God, and of the world partaking,
    " Of all that is, Man might the image beare.

God first made angels bodilesse, pure minds,
    Then other things, which mindlesse bodies be;
    Last, He made Man, th' *horizon* 'twixt both kinds,
    In whom we doe the World's abridgement see.

Besides, this World below did need *one wight*,
    Which might thereof distinguish euery part;
    Make vse thereof, and take therein delight,
    And order things with industry and art:

Which also God might in His works admire,
    And here beneath, yeeld Him both praier and
        praise;
    As there, aboue, the holy angels quire
    Doth spread His glory with spirituall layes.

Lastly, the bruite, unreasonable wights,
　　Did want a *visible king* on them to raigne:
　　And God, Himselfe thus to the World vnites,
　　That so the World might endlesse blisse obtaine.

In what manner the Soule is united to the Body

BUT how shall we this *union* well expresse?
　　Nought ties the *soule;* her subtiltie is such
　She moues the bodie, which she doth possesse,
　　Yet no part toucheth, but by *Vertue's* touch.

Then dwels shee not therein as in a tent,
　　Nor as a pilot in his ship doth sit;
　　Nor as the spider in his web is pent;
　　Nor as the waxe retaines the print in it;

Nor as a vessell water doth containe;
　　Nor as one liquor in another shed;
　　Nor as the heat doth in the fire remaine;
　　Nor as a voice throughout the ayre is spread:

But as the faire and cheerfull *Morning light,*
　　Doth here and there her siluer beames impart,
　　And in an instant doth herselfe vnite
　　To the transparent ayre, in all, and part:

Still resting whole, when blowes th' ayre diuide;
  Abiding pure, when th' ayre is most corrupted;
  Throughout the ayre, her beams dispersing wide,
  And when the ayre is tost, not interrupted:

So doth the piercing *Soule* the body fill,
  Being all in all, and all in part diffus'd;
  Indiuisible, incorruptible still,
  Not forc't, encountred, troubled or confus'd.

And as the *sunne* aboue, the light doth bring,
  Though we behold it in the ayre below;
  So from th' Eternall Light the *Soule* doth spring,
  Though in the body she her powers doe show.

HOW THE SOUL DOTH EXERCISE HER POWERS IN THE BODY

B UT *as* the world's *sunne* doth effects beget,
    Diuers, in diuers places euery day;
  Here *Autumnes* temperature, there *Summer's* heat,
  Here flowry *Spring-tide*, and there *Winter* gray:

Eere *Euen*, there *Morne*, here *Noone*, there *Day*,
    there *Night;*
  Melts wax, dries clay, mak[e]s flowrs, som
    quick, som dead;
  Makes the *More* black, and th' *Europæan* white,
  Th' *American* tawny, and th' *East-Indian* red:

So in our little World: this *soule* of ours,
  Being onely one, and to one body tyed,
  Doth vse, on diuers obiects diuers powers,
  And so are her effects diuersified.

THE VEGETATIUE OR QUICKENING POWER

H ER *quick'ning* power in euery liuing part,
      Doth as a nurse, or as a mother serue;
  And doth employ her *oeconomicke art*,
  And busie care, her houshold to preserue.

Here she *attracts*, and there she doth *retaine*,
  There she *decocts*, and doth the food prepare;
  There she *distributes* it to euery vaine,
  There she *expels* what she may fitly spare.

This power to *Martha* may comparèd be,
  Which busie was, the *houshold-things* to doe;
  Or to a *Dryas*, liuing in a tree:
  For euen to trees this power is proper too.

And though the Soule may not this power extend
  Out of the body, but still vse it there;
  She hath a power which she abroad doth send,
  Which views and searcheth all things euery
    where.

The power of Sense

T HIS *power is* Sense, which from abroad doth
     bring
The *colour, taste,* and *touch,* and *sent,* and *sound ;*
The *quantitie,* and *shape* of euery thing
Within th' Earth's center, or Heauen's circle
    found.

This power, in parts made fit, fit obiects takes,
    Yet not the things, but forms of things receiues ;
As when a seale in waxe impression makes,
    The print therein, but not it selfe it leaues.

And though things sensible be numberlesse,
    But onely fiue the *Senses'* organs be ;
And in those fiue, all things their formes ex-
    presse,
Which we can *touch, taste, feele,* or *heare,* or *see.*

These are the windows throgh the which she
    views
The *light of knowledge,* which is life's loadstar :
" And yet while she these spectacles doth vse,
" Oft worldly things seeme greater then they are.

SIGHT

FIRST, the two *eyes* that haue the *seeing* power,
Stand as one watchman, spy, or sentinell;
Being plac'd aloft, within the head's high tower;
And though both see, yet both but one thing tell.

These mirrors take into their little space
The formes of *moone* and *sun*, and euery *starre ;*
Of euery body and of euery place,
Which with the World's wide armes embracèd
are :

Yet their best obiect, and their noblest vse,
Hereafter in another World will be ;
When God in them shall heauenly light infuse,
That face to face they may their *Maker* see.

Here are they guides, which doe the body lead,
Which else would stumble in eternal night;
Here in this world they do much knowledge
read,
And are the casements which admit most light :

They are her farthest reaching instrument,
Yet they no beames vnto their obiects send ;
- But all the rays are from their obiects sent,
And in the *eyes* with pointed angles end :

If th' obiects be farre off, the rayes doe meet
   In a sharpe point, and so things seeme but small ;
If they be neere, their rayes doe spread and fleet,
   And make broad points, that things seeme great
      withall.

Lastly, nine things to *Sight* requirèd are ;
   The *power* to see, the *light*, the *visible* thing,
Being not too *small*, too *thin*, too *nigh*, too *farre*,
   Cleare space, and *time*, the forme distinct to
      bring.

Thus we see how the *Soule* doth vse the eyes,
   As instruments of her quicke power of sight ;
Hence do th' Arts *opticke* and faire *painting* rise :
   Painting, which doth all gentle minds delight.

HEARING

NOW let vs heare how she the *Eares* imployes :
      Their office is the troubled ayre to take,
Which in their mazes formes a sound or noyse,
   Whereof her selfe doth true distinction make.

These wickets of the *Soule* are plac't on hie
   Because all sounds doe lightly mount aloft ;
And that they may not pierce too violently,
   They are delaied with turnes, and windings oft.

For should the voice directly strike the braine,
　It would astonish and confuse it much;
　Therfore these plaits and folds the sound re-
　　straine,
　That it the organ may more gently touch.

As streames, which with their winding banks doe
　　play,
　Stopt by their creeks, run softly through the
　　plaine;
　So in th' Eares' labyrinth the voice doth stray,
　And doth with easie motion touch the braine.

It is the slowest, yet the daintiest *sense;*
　For euen the *Eares* of such as haue no skill,
　Perceiue a discord, and conceiue offence;
　And knowing not what is good, yet find the ill.

And though this *sense* first gentle *Musicke* found,
　Her proper obiect is *the speech of men;*
　But that speech chiefely which God's heraulds
　　sound,
　When their tongs vtter what His Spirit did pen.

Our *Eyes* haue lids, our *Eares* still ope we see,
　Quickly to heare how euery tale is prooued;
　Our *Eyes* still moue, our *Eares* vnmoued bee,
　That though we hear quick we be not quickly
　　moued.

Thus by the organs of the *Eye* and *Eare*,
　The *Soule* with knowledge doth her selfe endue;
　" Thus she her prison, may with pleasure beare,
　" Hauing such prospects, all the world to view.

These conduit-pipes of knowledge feed the Mind,
　But th' other three attend the Body still;
　For by their seruices the *Soule* doth find,
　What things are to the body, good or ill.

TASTE

THE *bodie's* life with meats and ayre is fed,
　　Therefore the *soule* doth vse the *tasting* power,
In veines, which through the tongue and palate
　　spred,
Distinguish euery relish, sweet and sower.

This is the bodie's *nurse;* but since man's wit
　Found th' art of *cookery*, to delight his *sense ;*
　More bodies are consum'd and kild with it,
　Then with the sword, famine, or pestilence.

SMELLING

NEXT, in the nosthrils she doth vse the *smell:*
　　As God the *breath of life* in them did giue,
So makes He now this power in them to dwell,
To iudge all ayres, whereby we *breath* and *liue.*

This *sense* is also mistresse of an Art,
   Which to soft people sweete perfumes doth sell;
   Though this deare Art doth little good impart,
   "Sith they smell best, that doe of nothing smell.

And yet good *sents* doe purifie the braine,
   Awake the fancie, and the wits refine;
   Hence old *Deuotion*, *incense* did ordaine
   To make mens' spirits apt for thoughts diuine.

FEELING

L ASTLY, *the feeling power*, which is Life's
   root,
   Through euery liuing part it selfe doth shed;
   By sinewes, which extend from head to foot,
   And like a net, all ore the body spred.

Much like a subtill spider, which doth sit
   In middle of her web, which spreadeth wide;
   If ought doe touch the vtmost thred of it,
   Shee feeles it instantly on euery side.

By *Touch*, the first pure qualities we learne,
   Which quicken all things, *hote, cold, moist*, and
      dry ;
   By *Touch, hard, soft, rough, smooth*, we doe dis-
      cerne;
   By *Touch, sweet pleasure*, and *sharpe paine*, we try.

THESE are the outward instruments of Sense,
    These are the guards which euery thing
      must passe
Ere it approch the mind's intelligence,
Or touch the Fantasie, *Wit's looking-glasse.*

THE IMAGINATION OR COMMON SENSE

AND yet these porters, which all things admit,
    Themselues perceiue not, nor discerne the
      things;
One *common* power doth in the forehead sit,
Which all their proper formes together brings.

For all those *nerues,* which *spirits of Sence* doe
    beare,
    And to those outward organs spreading goe;
Vnited are, as in a center there,
    And there this power those sundry formes doth
    know.

Those outward organs present things receiue,
    This inward *Sense* doth absent things retaine;
    Yet straight transmits all formes shee doth per-
    ceiue,
Vnto a higher region of the *braine.*

The Fantasie

WHERE *Fantasie,* neere *hand-maid* to the
  mind,
Sits and beholds, and doth discerne them all;
Compounds in one, things diuers in their kind;
Compares the black and white, the great and
  small.

Besides, those single formes she doth esteeme,
  And in her ballance doth their values trie;
  Where some things good, and some things ill
    doe seem,
  And neutrall some, in her *fantasticke* eye.

This busie power is working day and night;
  For when the outward *senses* rest doe take,
  A thousand dreames, fantasticall and light,
  With fluttring wings doe keepe her still awake.

The Sensitiue Memorie

YET alwayes all may not afore her bee;
  Successiuely, she this and that intends;
  Therefore such formes as she doth cease to
    see,
  To *Memorie's* large volume shee commends.

The *lidger-booke* lies in the braine behinde,
  Like *Ianus'* eye, which in his poll was set;
  The *lay-man's tables, store-house of the mind,*
  Which doth remember much, and much forget.

Heere *Sense's apprehension*, end doth take;
  As when a stone is into water cast,
  One circle doth another circle make,
  Till the last circle touch the banke at last.

THE PASSIONS OF SENSE

B UT though the *apprehensiue power* doe pause,
  The *motiue* vertue then begins to moue;
  Which in the heart below doth PASSIONS cause,
  Ioy, griefe, and *feare,* and *hope,* and *hate,* and *loue.*

These passions haue a free commanding might,
  And diuers actions in our life doe breed;
  For, all acts done without true Reason's light,
  Doe from the passion of the *Sense* proceed.

But sith the *braine* doth lodge the powers of *Sense,*
  How makes it in the heart those passions spring?
  The mutuall loue, the kind intelligence
  'Twixt heart and braine, this *sympathy* doth
    bring.

From the kind heat, which in the heart doth raigne,
    The *spirits* of life doe their begining take;
    These *spirits* of life ascending to the braine,
    When they come there, the *spirits of Sense* do
        make.

These *spirits of Sense*, in Fantasie's High Court,
    Iudge of the formes of *obiects*, ill or well;
    And so they send a good or ill report
    Downe to the heart, where all affections dwell.

If the report bee *good*, it causeth *loue*,
    And longing *hope*, and well-assurèd *ioy:*
    If it bee *ill*, then doth it *hatred* moue,
    And trembling *feare*, and vexing *griefe's* annoy.

Yet were these naturall affections good:
    (For they which want them, *blockes* or *deuils* be)
    If *Reason* in her first perfection stood,
    That she might *Nature's* passions rectifie.

THE MOTION OF LIFE

BESIDES, another *motiue*-power doth rise
    Out of the heart; from whose pure blood
      do spring
The *vitall spirits;* which, borne in *arteries*,
Continuall motion to all parts doe bring.

The Locall Motion

THIS makes the pulses beat, and lungs respire,
  This holds the sinewes like a bridle's reines;
And makes the Body to aduance, retire,
  To turne or stop, as she them slacks, or
    straines.

Thus the *soule* tunes the *bodie's* instrument;
  These harmonies she makes with *life* and *sense;*
The organs fit are by the body lent,
  But th' actions flow from the *Soule's* influence.

The intellectuall Powers of the Soule

BUT now I haue a *will*, yet want a *wit*,
  To expresse the working of the *wit* and
    will;
Which, though their root be to the body knit,
  Vse not the body, when they vse their skill.

These powers the nature of the *Soule declare*,
  For to man's *soule* these onely proper bee;
For on the Earth no other wights there are
  That haue these heauenly powers, but only we.

THE WIT OR UNDERSTANDING

THE WIT, the pupill of the *Soule's* cleare eye,
   And in man's world, the onely shining
   starre;
Lookes in the mirror of the Fantasie,
Where all the gatherings of the *Senses* are.

From thence this power the shapes of things ab-
   stracts,
   And them within her *passiue part* receiues;
   Which are enlightned by that part which *acts*,
   And so the formes of single things perceiues.

But after, by discoursing to and fro,
   Anticipating, and comparing things;
   She doth all vniversall natures know,
   And all *effects* into their *causes* brings.

REASON, VNDERSTANDING

WHEN she *rates* things and moues from
   ground to ground,
The name of *Reason* she obtaines by this;
But when by Reason she the truth hath found,
And *standeth fixt*, she VNDERSTANDING is.

Opinion, Judgement

WHEN her assent she *lightly* doth encline
    To either part, she is Opinion light:
But when she doth by principles define
    A certaine truth, she hath *true Judgement's*
      sight.

And as from *Senses*, *Reason's* worke doth spring,
    So many *reasons understanding* gaine;
And many *understandings*, *knowledge* bring;
    And by much *knowledge*, *wisdome* we obtaine.

So, many stayres we must ascend vpright
    Ere we attaine to *Wisdome's* high degree;
So doth this Earth eclipse our Reason's light.
    Which else (in instants) would like angels see.

Yet hath the *Soule* a dowrie naturall,
    And *sparkes of light*, some common things to
      see;
Not being a *blancke* where nought is writ at all,
    But what the writer will, may written be

For Nature in man's heart her lawes doth pen;
    Prescribing *truth* to *wit*, and *good* to *will;*
Which doe *accuse*, or else *excuse* all men,
    For euery thought or practise, good or ill:

And yet these sparkes grow almost infinite,
　　Making the World, and all therein their food;
　　As fire so spreads as no place holdeth it,
　　Being nourisht still, with new supplies of wood.

And though these sparkes were almost quencht
　　　　with sin,
　　Yet they whom that *Iust One* hath iustifide;
　　Haue them encreasd with heauenly light within,
　　And like the *widowe's oyle* still multiplide.

THE POWER OF WILL

A ND as this *wit* should goodnesse truely know,
　　　We haue a *Will*, which that true good
　　　　should chuse;
　　Though *Wil* do oft (when *wit* false formes doth
　　　　show)
　　Take *ill* for *good*, and *good* for *ill* refuse.

THE RELATIONS BETWIXT WIT AND WILL

W ILL puts in practice what the *Wit* deuiseth:
　　　Will euer acts, and *Wit* contemplates still;
　　And as from *Wit*, the power of *wisedome* riseth,
　　All other vertues daughters are of *Will*.

Will is the *prince*, and *Wit* the counseller,
   Which doth for common good in Counsell sit;
   And when *Wit* is resolu'd, *Will* lends her power
   To execute what is aduis'd by *Wit*.

Wit is the mind's chief iudge, which doth controule
   Of *Fancie's* Court the iudgements, false and
      vaine;
   Will holds the royall septer in the *soule*
   And on the passions of the heart doth raigne.

Will is as free as any emperour,
   Naught can restraine her *gentle* libertie;
   No tyrant, nor no torment, hath the power,
   To make vs *will*, when we vnwilling bee.

THE INTELLECTUALL MEMORIE

TO these high powers, a store-house doth per-
     taine,
   Where they all arts and generall reasons lay;
   Which in the *Soule*, euen after death, remaine
   And no *Lethæan* flood can wash away.

This is the *Soule*, and these her vertues bee;
   Which, though they haue their sundry proper
     ends,
   And one exceeds another in degree,
   Yet each on other mutually depends.

Our Wit is giuen, *Almighty God* to *know ;*
　　Our *Will* is giuen to *loue* Him, being *knowne ;*
　　But God could not be *known* to vs below,
　　But by His *workes* which through the sense are
　　　　shown.

And as the *Wit* doth reape the fruits of *Sense,*
　　So doth the *quickning* power the *senses feed ;*
　　Thus while they doe their sundry gifts dispence,
　　" The best, the seruice of the least doth need.

Euen so the King his Magistrates do serue,
　　Yet Commons feed both magistrate and king ;
　　The Commons' peace the magistrates preserue
　　By borrowed power, which from the Prince doth
　　　　spring.

The *quickning power* would *be,* and so would rest ;
　　The *Sense* would not *be* onely, but *be well ;*
　　But *Wit's* ambition longeth to the *best,*
　　For it desires in endlesse blisse to dwell.

And these three powers, three sorts of men doe
　　　　make :
　　For some, like plants, their veines doe onely fill ;
　　And some, like beasts, their senses' pleasure
　　　　take ;
　　And some, like angels, doe contemplate still.

Therefore the fables turnd some men to flowres,
  And others, did with bruitish formes inuest;
  And did of others, make celestiall powers,
  Like angels, which still trauell, yet still rest.

Yet these three powers are not three *soules*, but
    one;
  As one and two are both containd in *three;*
  Three being one number by it selfe alone:
  A shadow of the blessed Trinitie.

AN ACCLAMATION

O! what is Man (great Maker of mankind!)
    That Thou to him so great respect dost
    beare!
  That Thou adornst him with so bright a mind,
  Mak'st him a king, and euen an angel's peere!

O! what a liuely life, what heauenly power,
  What spreading vertue, what a sparkling fire!
  How great, how plentifull, how rich a dower
  Dost Thou within this dying flesh inspire!

Thou leau'st Thy print in other works of Thine,
  But Thy whole image Thou in Man hast writ;
  There cannot be a creature more diuine,
  Except (like Thee) it should be infinit.

But it exceeds man's thought, to thinke how hie
   God hath raisd *Man*, since *God a man* became;
   The angels doe admire this *Misterie*,
   And are astonisht when they view the same.

THAT THE SOULE IS IMMORTAL, AND CANNOT DIE

NOR hath He giuen these blessings for a day,
   Nor made them on the bodie's life depend;
   The *Soule* though made in time, *suruives for aye,*
   And though it hath beginning, sees no end.

Her onely *end*, is *neuer-ending* blisse;
   Which is, *th' eternall face of God to see;*
   Who *Last of Ends*, and *First of Causes*, is:
   And to doe this, she must *eternall* bee.

How senselesse then, and dead a soule hath hee,
   Which *thinks* his *soule* doth with his body die!
   Or *thinkes* not so, but so would haue it bee,
   That he might sinne with more securitie.

For though these light and vicious persons say,
   Our *Soule* is but a smoake, or ayrie blast;
   Which, during life, doth in our nostrils play,
   And when we die, doth turne to wind at last:

Although they say, '*Come let us eat and drinke*';
   Our life is but a sparke, which quickly dies;
   Though thus they *say*, they know not what to think,
   But in their minds ten thousand doubts arise.

Therefore no heretikes desire to spread
   Their light opinions, like these *Epicures:*
   For so the staggering thoughts are comfortèd,
   And other men's assent their doubt assures.

Yet though these men against their conscience
     striue,
   There are some sparkles in their flintie breasts
   Which cannot be extinct, but still reuiue;
   That though they would, they cannot quite bee
     beasts;

But who so makes a mirror of his mind,
   And doth with patience view himselfe therein,
   His *Soule's* eternitie shall clearely find,
   Though th' other beauties be defac't with sin.

Reason I

Drawne from the desire of Knowledge

FIRST *in Man's mind* we find an appetite
   To *learne* and *know the truth* of euery thing;
   Which is co-naturall, and borne with it,
   And from the *essence* of the *soule* doth spring.

With this *desire*, shee hath a natiue *might*
    To find out euery truth, if she had time;
    Th' innumerable effects to sort aright,
    And by degrees, from cause to cause to clime.

But sith our life so fast away doth slide,
    As doth a hungry eagle through the wind,
    Or as a ship transported with the tide;
    Which in their passage leaue no print behind;

Of which swift little time so much we spend,
    While some few things we through the sense doe
        straine;
    That our short race of life is at an end,
    Ere we the principles of skill attaine.

Or God (which to vaine ends hath nothing done)
    In vaine this *appetite* and *power* hath giuen;
    Or else our knowledge, which is here begun,
    Hereafter must bee perfected in heauen.

God neuer gaue a *power* to one whole kind,
    But most part of that kind did vse the same;
    Most eies haue perfect sight, though some be
        blind;
    Most legs can nimbly run, though some be
        lame:

But in this life no *soule* the truth can know
    So perfectly, as it hath power to doe;
    If then perfection be not found below,
    An higher place must make her mount thereto.

REASON II

DRAWN FROM THE MOTION OF THE SOULE

A *GAINE* how can shee but immortall bee?
    When with the motions of both *Will* and
      Wit,
    She still aspireth to eternitie,
    And neuer rests, till she attaine to it?

Water in conduit pipes, can rise no higher
    Then the wel-head, from whence it first doth
      spring:
    Then sith to eternall GOD shee doth aspire,
    Shee cannot be but an eternall thing.

" All mouing things to other things doe moue,
    " Of the same kind, which shews their nature
      such;
    So *earth* falls downe and *fire* doth mount aboue,
    Till both their proper elements doe touch.

The Soul compared to a Riuer

And as the moysture, which the thirstie earth
   Suckes from the sea, to fill her emptie veines,
   From out her wombe at last doth take a
      birth,
   And runs a *Nymph* along the grassie plaines:

Long doth shee stay, as loth to leaue the land,
   From whose soft side she first did issue make;
   Shee tastes all places, turnes to euery hand,
   Her flowry bankes vnwilling to forsake:

Yet *Nature* so her streames doth lead and carry,
   As that her course doth make no finall stay,
   Till she her selfe vnto the *Ocean* marry,
   Within whose watry bosome first she lay:

Euen so the *Soule* which in this earthly mold
   The Spirit of God doth secretly infuse;
   Because at first she doth the earth behold,
   And onely this materiall world she viewes:

At first her *mother-earth* she holdeth deare,
   And doth embrace the world and worldly things:
   She flies close by the ground, and houers here,
   And mounts not vp with her celestiall wings.

Yet vnder heauen she cannot light on ought
   That with her heauenly *nature* doth agree;
   She cannot rest, she cannot fix her thought,
   She cannot in this world contented bee:

For who did euer yet, in *honour, wealth,*
   Or *pleasure of the sense,* contentment find?
   Who euer ceasd to wish, when he had *health ?*
   Or hauing *wisedome* was not vext in mind?

Then as a *bee* which among weeds doth fall,
   Which seeme sweet flowers, with lustre fresh and
      gay;
   She lights on that, and this, and tasteth all,
   But pleasd with none, doth rise, and soare away;

So, when the *Soule* finds here no true content,
   And, like *Noah's* doue, can no sure footing take;
   She doth returne from whence she first was sent,
   And flies to *Him* that first her wings did make.

Wit, seeking *Truth,* from cause to cause ascends,
   And neuer rests, till it the *first* attaine:
   Will, seeking *Good,* finds many middle ends,
   But neuer stayes, till it the *last* doe gaine.

Now God, the *Truth,* and *First of Causes* is:
   God is the *Last Good End,* which lasteth still;
   Being *Alpha* and *Omega* nam'd for this;
   Alpha to *Wit, Omega* to the *Will.*

Sith then her heauenly kind shee doth bewray,
  In that to God she doth directly moue;
  And on no mortall thing can make her stay,
  She cannot be from hence, but from *aboue*.

And yet this *First True Cause,* and *Last Good End,*
  Shee cannot heere so *well,* and *truely* see;
  For this perfection shee must yet attend,
  Till to her *Maker* shee espousèd bee.

As a *king's* daughter, being in person sought
  Of diuers princes, who doe neighbour neere;
  On none of them can fixe a constant thought,
  Though shee to all doe lend a gentle eare:

Yet she can loue a forraine *emperour,*
  Whom of great worth and power she heares to be;
  If she be woo'd but by *embassadour,*
  Or but his *letters,* or his pictures see:

For well she knowes, that when she shalbe brought
  Into the *kingdome* where her *Spouse* doth raigne;
  Her eyes shall see what she conceiu'd in thought,
  Himselfe, his state, his glory, and his traine.

So while the *virgin Soule* on *Earth* doth stay,
  She woo'd and tempted is ten thousand wayes,
  By these great powers, which on the *Earth* beare
      sway;
  The *wisdom of the World, wealth, pleasure, praise:*

With these sometime she doth her time beguile,
   These doe by fits her Fantasie possesse;
   But she distastes them all within a while,
   And in the sweetest finds a tediousnesse.

But if upon the World's Almighty King
   She once doe fixe her humble louing thought;
   Who by His *picture*, drawne in euery thing,
   And *sacred messages*, her *loue* hath sought;

Of Him she thinks, she cannot thinke too much;
   This hony tasted still, is euer sweet;
   The pleasure of her rauisht thought is such,
   As almost here, she with her blisse doth
      meet:

But when in Heauen she shall His *Essence* see,
   This is her *soueraigne good, and perfect blisse:*
   Her longings, wishings, hopes all finisht be,
   Her ioyes are full, her motions rest in this:

There is she crownd with garlands of *content*,
   There doth she manna eat, and nectar drinke;
   That Presence doth such high delights present,
   As neuer tongue could speake, nor heart could
      thinke.

Reason III

From Contempt of Death in the better Sort of Spirits

FOR *this* the better *Soules* doe oft despise
The bodie's death, and doe it oft desire;
For when on ground, the burdened ballance lies
The emptie part is lifted vp the higher:

But if the bodie's death the *soule* should kill,
Then death must needs *against her nature* bee;
And were it so, all *soules* would flie it still,
" For Nature hates and shunnes her contrary.

For all things else, which Nature makes to bee,
Their *being* to preserue, are chiefly taught;
And though some things desire a change to see,
Yet neuer thing did long to turne to naught.

If then by death the *soule* were quenchèd quite,
She could not thus against her nature runne;
Since euery senselesse thing, by Nature's light,
Doth preservation seeke, destruction shunne.

Nor could the World's best spirits so much erre,
If death tooke all — that they should all agree,
Before this life, their *honour* to preferre;
For what is praise to things that nothing bee?

Againe, if by the bodie's prop she stand;
　　If on the bodie's life, her life depend;
　　As *Meleager's* on the fatall brand, —
　　The bodie's good shee onely would intend:

We should not find her half so braue and bold,
　　To leade it to the Warres and to the seas;
　　To make it suffer watchings, hunger, cold,
　　When it might feed with plenty, rest with
　　　　ease.

Doubtlesse all *Soules* have a suruiuing thought;
　　Therefore of death we thinke with quiet mind;
　　But if we thinke of *being turn'd to nought*,
　　A trembling horror in our *soules* we find.

REASON IV

FROM THE FEARE OF DEATH IN THE WICKED SOULES

A *ND as* the better spirit, when shee doth beare
　　A scorne of death, doth shew she cannot
　　die;
So when the wicked *Soule* Death's face doth
　　feare,
Euen then she proues her owne eternitie.

For when Death's forme appeares, she feareth not
　　An vtter quenching or extinguishment;
　　She would be glad to meet with such a lot,
　　That so she might all future ill preuent:

But shee doth doubt what after may befall;
　　For Nature's law accuseth her within;
　　And saith, 'Tis true that is affirm'd by all,
　　That after death there is a paine for sin.

Then she which hath bin hud-winkt from her birth,
　　Doth first her selfe within Death's mirror see;
　　And when her body doth returne to earth,
　　She first takes care, how she alone shall bee.

Who euer sees these irreligious men,
　　With burthen of a sicknesse weake and faint;
　　But heares them talking of Religion then,
　　And vowing of their *soules* to euery saint?

When was there euer cursèd *atheist* brought
　　Vnto the *gibbet*, but he did adore
　　That blessed Power, which he had set at nought,
　　Scorn'd and blasphemèd all his life before?

These light vaine persons still are drunke and mad,
　　With surfettings and pleasures of their youth;
　　But at their deaths they are fresh, sober, sad;
　　Then they discerne, and then they speake the
　　　　truth.

If then all *Soules*, both good and bad, doe teach,
  With generall voice, that *soules* can neuer die;
  'Tis not man's flattering glosse, but *Nature's speech*,
  Which, like *God's* Oracle, can neuer lie.

REASON V

FROM THE GENERALL DESIRE OF IMMORTALITIE

H*ENCE springs* that vniuersall strong desire,
  Which all men haue of Immortalitie:
Not some few spirits vnto this thought aspire,
But all mens' minds in this vnited be.

Then this desire of Nature is not vaine,
  " She couets not impossibilities;
  " Fond thoughts may fall into some idle braine,
  " But one *assent* of all, is euer wise.

From hence that generall care and study springs,
  That *launching* and *progression of the mind ;*
  Which all men haue so much, of future things,
  That they no ioy doe in the present find.

From this desire, that maine desire proceeds,
  Which all men haue suruiuing Fame to gaine;
  By *tombes*, by *bookes*, by memorable *deeds :*
  For she that this desires, doth still remaine.

Hence lastly, springs care of posterities,
    For things their kind would euerlasting make;
    Hence is it that old men do plant young trees,
    The fruit whereof another age shall take.

If we these rules vnto our selues apply,
    And view them by reflection of the mind;
    All these true notes of immortalitie
    In our *heart's tables* we shall written find.

REASON VI

FROM THE VERY DOUBT AND DISPUTATION OF IMMORTALITIE

AND though some impious wits do questions moue,
    And doubt if *Soules* immortall be, or no ;
    That *doubt* their immortalitie doth proue,
    Because they seeme immortall things to know.

For he which reasons on both parts doth bring,
    Doth some things mortall, some immortall call;
    Now, if himselfe were but a mortall thing,
    He could not iudge immortall things at all.

For when we iudge, our minds we mirrors make:
    And as those glasses which materiall bee,
    Formes of materiall things doe onely take,
    For *thoughts* or *minds* in them we cannot see;

So, when we God and angels do conceiue,
    And thinke of *truth*, which is eternall too;
    Then doe our minds immortall formes receiue,
    Which if they mortall were, they could not
        doo:

And as, if beasts conceiu'd what Reason were,
    And that conception should distinctly show,
    They should the name of *reasonable* beare;
    For without *Reason*, none could *Reason* know:

So, when the *Soule* mounts with so high a wing,
    As of eternall things she *doubts* can moue;
    Shee proofes of her eternitie doth bring,
    Euen when she striues the contrary to proue.

For euen the *thought* of immortalitie,
    Being an act done without the bodie's ayde;
    Shewes, that her selfe alone could moue and
        bee,
    Although the body in the graue were layde.

THAT THE SOULE CANNOT BE DESTROYED

A ND if her selfe she can so liuely moue,
    And neuer need a forraine helpe to take;
Then must her motion euerlasting proue,
" Because her selfe she neuer can forsake.

Her Cause ceaseth not

But though corruption cannot touch the minde,
   By any cause that from it selfe may spring;
   Some outward cause Fate hath perhaps de-
      signd,
   Which to the *Soule* may vtter quenching bring.

She hath no Contrary

Perhaps her cause may cease, and she may die;
   God is her *cause*, His *Word* her Maker was;
   Which shall stand fixt for all eternitie
   When Heauen and Earth shall like a shadow
      passe.

Perhaps some thing repugnant to her kind,
   By strong *antipathy*, the *Soule* may kill;
   But what can be *contrary* to the minde,
   Which holds all *contraries* in concord still?

She lodgeth heat, and cold, and moist, and dry,
   And life, and death, and peace, and war to-
      gether;
   Ten thousand fighting things in her doe lye,
   Yet neither troubleth, or disturbeth either.

SHEE CANNOT DIE FOR WANT OF FOOD

Perhaps for want of food the *soule* may pine;
 But that were strange, sith all things *bad* and
  good,
 Sith all God's creature's *mortall* and *diuine*,
 Sith *God Himselfe*, is her eternall food.

Bodies are fed with things of mortall kind,
 And so are subiect to mortalitie;
 But *Truth* which is eternall, feeds the mind;
 The *Tree of life*, which will not let her die.

VIOLENCE CANNOT DESTROY HER

Yet violence, perhaps the *Soule* destroyes:
 As lightning, or the *sun-beames* dim the sight;
 Or as a thunder-clap, or cannons' noyse,
 The power of hearing doth astonish quite.

But high perfection to the *Soule* it brings,
 T' encounter things most excellent and high;
 For, when she views the best and greatest things
 They do not hurt, but rather cleare her eye,

Besides,—as *Homer's gods* 'gainst armies stand,—
 Her subtill forme can through all dangers slide;
 Bodies are captiue, *minds* endure no band,
 " And Will is free, and can no force abide.

TIME CANNOT DESTROY HER

But lastly, *Time* perhaps at last hath power
   To spend her liuely powers, and quench her
     light;
   But old god *Saturne* which doth all deuoure,
   Doth cherish her, and still augment her might.

Heauen waxeth old, and all the *spheres* aboue
   Shall one day faint, and their swift motion stay;
   And *Time* it selfe in time shall cease to moue;
   Onely the Soule suruiues, and liues for aye.

" Our Bodies, euery footstep that they make,
   " March towards death, vntill at last they die;
   " Whether we worke, or play, or sleepe, or wake,
   " Our life doth passe, and with *Time's* wings doth
     flie:

But to the *Soule* Time doth perfection giue,
   And ads fresh lustre to her beauty still;
   And makes her in eternall youth to liue,
   Like her which nectar to the gods doth fill.

The more she liues, the more she feeds on *Truth;*
   The more she feeds, her *strength* doth more in-
     crease :
   And what is *strength*, but an effect of *youth?*
   Which if *Time* nurse, how can it euer cease?

OBJECTIONS AGAINST THE IMMORTALITIE OF
THE SOULE

B*UT now* these *Epicures* begin to smile,
　　And say, my doctrine is more false then
　　　true;
And that I fondly doe my selfe beguile,
While these receiu'd opinions I ensue.

OBJECTION I

F*OR* what, say they, doth not the *Soule* waxe old?
　　How comes it then that agèd men doe dote;
And that their braines grow sottish, dull and cold,
Which were in youth the onely spirits of note?

What? are not *Soules* within themselues corrupted?
　　How can there idiots then by nature bee?
　　How is it that some wits are interrupted,
That now they dazeled are, now clearely see?

ANSWERE

T*HESE questions* make a subtill argument,
　　To such as thinke both *sense* and *reason* one;
To whom nor agent, from the instrument,
Nor power of working, from the work is known.

But they that know that wit can shew no skill,
 But when she things in *Sense's glasse* doth view;
 Doe know, if accident this glasse doe spill,
 It *nothing sees*, or *sees the false for true*.

For, if that region of the tender braine,
 Where th' inward sense of Fantasie should sit,
 And the outward senses gatherings should retain,
 By Nature, or by chance, become vnfit;

Either at first vncapable it is,
 And so few things, or none at all receiues;
 Or mard by accident, which haps amisse
 And so amisse it euery thing perceiues.

Then, as a cunning prince that vseth *spyes*,
 If they returne no newes doth nothing know;
 But if they make aduertisement of lies,
 The Prince's Counsel all awry doe goe.

Euen so the *Soule* to such a body knit,
 Whose inward senses vndisposèd be,
 And to receiue the formes of things vnfit;
 Where nothing is brought in, can nothing see.

This makes the idiot, which hath yet a mind,
 Able to *know* the truth, and *chuse* the good;
 If she such figures in the braine did find,
 As might be found, if it in temper stood.

But if a *phrensie* doe possesse the braine,
    It so disturbs and blots the formes of things;
    As Fantasie prooues altogether vaine,
    And to the Wit no true relation brings.

Then doth the Wit, admitting all for true,
    Build fond conclusions on those idle grounds;
    Then doth it flie the good, and ill pursue,
    Beleeuing all that this false *spie* propounds.

But purge the humors, and the rage appease,
    Which this distemper in the fansie wrought;
    Then shall the *Wit*, which never had disease,
    Discourse, and iudge discreetly, as it ought.

So, though the clouds eclipse the *sunne's* faire light,
    Yet from his face they doe not take one beame;
    So haue our eyes their perfect power of sight,
    Euen when they looke into a troubled streame.

Then these defects in *Senses'* organs bee,
    Not in the *soule* or in her working might;
    She cannot lose her perfect power to see,
    Thogh mists and clouds do choke her window
        light.

These imperfections then we must impute,
    Not to the agent but the instrument;
    We must not blame *Apollo*, but his lute,
    If false accords from her false strings be sent.

The *Soule* in all hath one intelligence;
   Though too much moisture in an infant's braine,
   And too much drinesse in an old man's sense,
   Cannot the prints of outward things retaine:

Then doth the *Soule* want worke, and idle sit,
   And this we *childishnesse* and *dotage* call;
   Yet hath she then a quicke and actiue Wit,
   If she had stuffe and tooles to worke withall:

For, giue her organs fit, and obiects faire;
   Giue but the aged man, the young man's sense;
   Let but *Medea*, *Æson's* youth repaire,
   And straight she shewes her wonted excellence.

As a good harper stricken farre in yeares,
   Into whose cunning hand the gowt is fall;
   All his old crotchets in his braine he beares,
   But on his harpe playes ill, or not at all.

But if *Apollo* takes his gowt away,
   That hee his nimble fingers may apply;
   Apollo's selfe will enuy at his play,
   And all the world applaud his minstralsie.

Then *dotage* is no weaknesse of the mind,
   But of the *Sense;* for if the mind did waste,
   In all old men we should this wasting find,
   When they some certaine terme of yeres had
       past:

But most of them, euen to their dying howre,
  Retaine a mind more liuely, quicke, and
    strong;
  And better vse their vnderstanding power,
  Then when their braines were warm, and lims
    were yong.

For, though the body wasted be and weake,
  And though the leaden forme of earth it
    beares;
  Yet when we heare that halfe-dead body speake,
  We oft are rauisht to the heauenly *spheares*.

OBJECTION II

YET say these men, If all her organs die,
  Then hath the *soule* no power her powers to
    vse;
  So, in a sort, her powers extinct doe lie,
  When vnto *act* shee cannot them reduce.

And if her powers be dead, then what is shee?
  For sith from euery thing some powers do
    spring,
  And from those powers, some *acts* proceeding
    bee,
  Then kill both *power* and *act*, and kill the *thing*.

ANSWERE

D *OUBTLESSE* the bodie's death when once it
dies,
The instruments of sense and life doth kill;
So that she cannot vse those faculties,
Although their root rest in her substance still.

But (as the body liuing) *Wit* and *Will*
Can *iudge* and *chuse*, without the bodie's ayde;
Though on such obiects they are working still,
As through the bodie's organs are conuayde:

So, when the body serues her turne no more,
And all her *Senses* are extinct and gone,
She can discourse of what she learn'd before,
In heauenly contemplations, all alone.

So, if one man well on a lute doth play,
And haue good horsemanship, and Learning's
skill;
Though both his lute and horse we take away,
Doth he not keep his former learning still?

He keepes it doubtlesse, and can vse it to[o];
And doth both th' other *skils* in power retaine;
And can of both the proper actions doe,
If with his lute or horse he meet againe.

So (though the instruments by which we liue,
　And view the world, the bodie's death doe
　　kill;)
　Yet with the body they shall all reuiue,
　And all their wonted offices fulfill.

OBJECTION III

B*UT how*, till then, shall she herselfe imploy?
　　Her spies are dead which brought home
　　　newes before;
　What she hath got and keepes, she may enioy,
　But she hath meanes to vnderstand no more.

Then what do those poore *soules*, which nothing
　　get?
　Or what doe those which get, and cannot keepe?
　Like buckets bottomlesse, which all out-let
　Those *Soules*, for want of exercise, must sleepe.

ANSWERE

S*EE how* man's *Soule* against it selfe doth
　　striue:
　Why should we not haue other meanes to know?
　As children while within the wombe they liue,
　Feed by the nauill: here they feed not so.

These children, if they had some vse of sense,
>   And should by chance their mothers' talking
>   heare;
>   That in short time they shall come forth from
>   thence,
>   Would feare their birth more then our death we
>   feare.

They would cry out, 'If we this place shall
>   leaue,
>   Then shall we breake our tender nauill strings;
>   How shall we then our nourishment receiue,
>   Sith our sweet food no other conduit brings?'

And if a man should to these babes reply,
>   That into this faire world they shall be brought;
>   Where they shall see the Earth, the Sea, the
>   Skie,
>   The glorious Sun, and all that God hath
>   wrought:

That there ten thousand dainties they shall meet,
>   Which by their mouthes they shall with pleasure
>   take;
>   Which shall be cordiall too, as wel as sweet,
>   And of their little limbes, tall bodies make:

This would they thinke a fable, euen as we
  Doe thinke the *story* of the *Golden Age;*
  Or as some sensuall spirits amongst vs bee,
  Which hold the *world to come, a fainèd stage:*

Yet shall these infants after find all true,
  Though then thereof they nothing could con-
    ceiue;
  As soone as they are borne, the world they
    view,
  And with their mouthes, the nurses'-milke re-
    ceiue.

So, when the *Soule* is borne (for Death is nought
  But the *Soule's* birth, and so we should it
    call)
  Ten thousand things she sees beyond her
    thought,
  And in an vnknowne manner knowes them all.

Then doth she see by spectacles no more,
  She heares not by report of double spies;
  Her selfe in instants doth all things explore,
  For each thing present, and before her, lies.

Objection IV

B *UT still* this crue with questions me pursues :
　　If *soules* deceas'd (say they) still liuing
　　　bee ;
Why do they not return, to bring vs newes
Of that strange world, where they such wonders
　　see ?

Answere

F *OND men !* If we beleeue that men doe liue
　　Vnder the *Zenith* of both frozen *Poles*,
Though none come thence aduertisement to
　　giue ;
Why beare we not the like faith of our *soules ?*

The *soule* hath here on Earth no more to doe,
　　Then we haue businesse in our mother's wombe ;
　　What child doth couet to returne thereto ?
　　Although all children first from thence do come ?

But as *Noah's* pidgeon, which return'd no more,
　　Did shew, she footing found, for all the Flood ;
　　So when good soules, departed through Death's
　　　dore,
　　Come not againe, it shewes their dwelling good.

And doubtlesse, such a *soule* as vp doth mount,
 And doth appeare before her Maker's Face;
 Holds this vile world in such a base account,
 As she looks down, and scorns this wretched
  place.

But such as are detruded downe to He
 Either for shame, they still themselues retire;
 Or tyed in chaines, they in close prison dwell,
 And cannot come, although they much desire.

OBJECTION V

WELL, *well*, say these vaine spirits, though
  vaine it is
To thinke our *Soules* to Heauen or Hell to
 goe,
Politike men haue thought it not amisse,
To spread this *lye*, to make men vertuous so.

ANSWERE

DOE *you* then thinke this *morall vertue* good?
 I thinke you doe, euen for your priuate
  gaine;
For Common-wealths by *vertue* euer stood,
And common good the priuate doth containe.

If then this *vertue* you doe loue so well,
    Haue you no meanes, her practise to main-
        taine;
    But you this lye must to the people tell,
    That good *Soules* liue in ioy, and ill in paine?

Must *vertue* be preseruèd by a *lye?*
    Vertue and *Truth* do euer best agree;
    By this it seemes to be a veritie,
    Sith the effects so good and vertuous bee.

For, as the deuill father is of lies,
    So vice and mischiefe doe his lyes ensue;
    Then this good doctrine did not he deuise,
    But made this *lye*, which saith it is not true.

THE GENERALL CONSENT OF ALL

FOR *how* can that be false, which euery tongue
    Of euery mortall man affirmes for true?
    Which truth hath in all ages been so strong,
    As lodestone-like, all hearts it euer drew.

For, not the *Christian*, or the *Iew* alone,
    The *Persian*, or the *Turke*, acknowledge this;
    This mysterie to the wild *Indian* knowne,
    And to the *Canniball* and *Tartar* is.

This rich *Assyrian* drugge growes euery where;
    As common in the *North*, as in the *East;*
    This doctrine does not enter by the *eare*,
    But of it selfe is natiue in the breast.

None that acknowledge God, or prouidence,
    Their *Soule's* eternitie did euer doubt;
    For all *Religion* takes her root from hence,
    Which no poore naked nation liues without.

For sith the World for Man created was,
    (For onely Man the vse thereof doth know)
    If man doe perish like a withered grasse,
    How doth God's Wisedom order things below?

And if that Wisedom still wise ends propound,
    Why made He man, of other creatures King?
    When (if he perish here) there is not found
    In all the world so poor and vile a thing?

If death do quench vs quite, we haue great
      wrong,
    Sith for our seruice all things else were wrought;
    That *dawes*, and *trees*, and *rocks*, should last so
      long,
    When we must in an instant passe to nought.

But blest be that *Great Power*, that hath vs
    blest
    With longer life then Heauen or Earth can haue;
    Which hath infus'd into our mortall breast
    Immortall powers, not subiect to the graue.

For though the Soule doe seeme her graue to
    beare,
    And in this world is almost buried quick;
    We haue no cause the bodie's death to feare,
    For when the shell is broke, out comes a
    chick.

Three Kinds of Life answerable to the three Powers of the Soule

FOR as the *soule's essentiall* powers are three,
    The *quickning power*, the *power of sense* and
    reason;
    Three kinds of life to her designèd bee,
    Which perfect these three powers in their due
    season.

The first life, in the mother's wombe is spent,
    Where she her *nursing power* doth onely vse;
    Where, when she finds defect of nourishment,
    Sh' expels her body, and this world she viewes.

This we call *Birth;* but if the child could speake,
    He *Death* would call it; and of Nature plaine,
    That she would thrust him out naked and weake,
    And in his passage pinch him with such paine.

Yet, out he comes, and in this world is plac't,
    Where all his *Senses* in perfection bee;
    Where he finds flowers to smell, and fruits to
        taste;
    And sounds to heare, and sundry formes to see.

When he hath past some time vpon this stage,
    His *Reason* then a little seemes to wake;
    Which, thogh she spring, when sense doth fade
        with age,
    Yet can she here no perfect practise make.

Then doth th' aspiring *Soule* the body leaue,
    Which we call *Death;* but were it knowne to all,
    What *life* our *soules* do by this *death* receiue,
    Men would it *birth* or *gaole deliuery* call.

In this third life, Reason will be so bright,
    As that her sparke will like the *sun-beames*
        shine;
    And shall of God enioy the reall sight.
    Being still increast by influence diuine.

AN ACCLAMATION

O IGNORANT poor man! what dost thou beare
   Lockt vp within the casket of thy brest?
   What iewels, and what riches hast thou there!
   What heauenly treasure in so weake a chest!

Looke in thy *soule*, and thou shalt *beauties* find,
   Like those which drownd *Narcissus* in the flood:
   Honour and *Pleasure* both are in thy mind,
   And all that in the world is counted *Good*.

Thinke of her worth, and think that God did meane,
   This worthy mind should worthy things im-
      brace;
   Blot not her beauties with thy thoughts vnclean,
   Nor her dishonour with thy passions base;

Kill not her *quickning power* with surfettings,
   Mar not her *Sense* with sensualitie;
   Cast not her serious wit on idle things:
   Make not her free-*will*, slaue to vanitie.

And when thou think'st of her *eternitie*,
   Thinke not that *Death* against her nature is,
   Thinke it a *birth;* and when thou goest to die,
   Sing like a swan, as if thou went'st to blisse.

And if thou, like a child, didst feare before,
  Being in the darke, where thou didst nothing see;
  Now I haue broght thee *torch-light*, feare no
    more;
  Now when thou diest, thou canst not hud-winkt
    be.

And thou my *Soule*, which turn'st thy curious eye,
  To view the beames of thine owne forme diuine;
  Know, that thou canst know nothing perfectly,
  While thou art clouded with this flesh of mine.

Take heed of *ouer-weening*, and compare
  Thy peacock's feet with thy gay peacock's traine;
  Study the best, and highest things that are,
  But of thy selfe an humble thought retaine.

Cast downe thy selfe, and onely striue to raise
  The glory of thy Maker's sacred Name;
  Vse all thy powers, that Blessed Power to praise,
  Which giues thee power to *bee*, and *vse the*
    same.

FINIS